Research
Shortcuts

Other Books by Judi Kesselman-Turkel and Franklynn Peterson:

BOOKS IN THIS SERIES

The Grammar Crammer: How to Write Perfect Sentences
Note-Taking Made Easy
Secrets to Writing Great Papers
Spelling Simplified
Study Smarts: How to Learn More in Less Time
Test-Taking Strategies
The Vocabulary Builder: The Practically Painless Way to a Larger Vocabulary

OTHER COAUTHORED BOOKS FOR ADULTS

The Author's Handbook
The Do-It-Yourself Custom Van Book (with Dr. Frank Konishi)
Eat Anything Exercise Diet (with Dr. Frank Konishi)
Good Writing
Homeowner's Book of Lists
The Magazine Writer's Handbook

COAUTHORED BOOKS FOR CHILDREN

I Can Use Tools
Vans

BY JUDI KESSELMAN-TURKEL

Stopping Out: A Guide to Leaving College and Getting Back In

BY FRANKLYNN PETERSON

The Build-It-Yourself Furniture Catalog
Children's Toys You Can Build Yourself
Freedom from Fibromyalgia (with Nancy Selfridge, M.D.)
Handbook of Lawn Mower Repair
Handbook of Snowmobile Maintenance and Repair
How to Fix Damn Near Everything
How to Improve Damn Near Everything around Your Home

Research Shortcuts

revised edition

Judi Kesselman-Turkel and Franklynn Peterson

The University of Wisconsin Press

The University of Wisconsin Press
1930 Monroe Street
Madison, Wisconsin 53711

www.wisc.edu/wisconsinpress/

3 Henrietta Street
London WC2E 8LU, England

5   4   3   2   1

Printed in the United States of America

Library of Congress Cataloging-in-Publication Data
Kesselman-Turkel, Judi.
    Research shortcuts / Judi Kesselman-Turkel and Franklynn
    Peterson.—Rev. ed.
    p. cm.
    Previous ed.: Chicago : Contemporary Books, © 1982.
    ISBN 0-299-19164-8 (pbk. : alk. paper)
    1. Report writing. 2. Research. I. Peterson, Franklynn. II. Title.
LB2369.K45   2003
808'.02—dc21   2003045829

CONTENTS

PART IV: GETTING INTO UNEXPLORED TERRITORY: SHORTCUTS THAT REACH THE EXPERTS

PART V: ROADMAP FOR A GRADE-A PAPER: USING YOUR RESEARCH MATERIALS

INTRODUCTION

We live and work in a college town alongside 40,000 college students. In researching the eighteen books and 1,000 or so magazine articles we've written, we often sit right alongside college students struggling with their own research.

Struggling is the word. While one of us spent two weeks in the medical library getting facts and figures for a 200-page book on diet and exercise, she watched a grad student winding down six weeks of research for a term paper. And while the other of us spent a day in the education library to gather enough information for a twenty-page typewritten article, he saw a student check out a week's worth of reading for a five-page essay.

Back in school, we weren't any different. Because nobody had told us about research shortcuts, we wrestled just as long with school research—and never sharpened our techniques or thought about using them to help solve career decisions or answer health questions. By now, researching has become so fast and effortless that we use it to find solutions for personal questions as well as on the job. After all these years, we can go right to the most valuable tools and materials almost instantly. We've learned to cut hours, sometimes days, off our research time. And we've discovered that for certain projects, answers are found easiest outside of any library.

There are already lots of good guides on the bookshelves that list and explain most of the basic library reference tools. Some of these guides are hundreds of pages long. We don't intend to duplicate their information. Instead, we'll share with you the techniques and shortcuts that years of research time have taught us, so that you can find your way like a pro to the best and fastest resources for your own projects.

PART I

MAPPING YOUR ROUTE: SHORTCUTS TO TAKE BEFORE YOU GO ANYWHERE

SHORTCUT 1

Decide Who You're Researching For

The kind of information you collect when you research depends first and foremost on *why* you're researching. Even if you go to the same information sources for two different research projects, you'll probably be looking for different kinds of data. For example, if you were looking for a summer camp job for yourself, you'd go to the same sources as if you were writing a newspaper article on summer camp jobs. But in the first instance, you have to consider only your own likes and needs. For the article, you have to take into account the likes and needs of all the readers.

For another example, if you have to write a paper on civil rights, you're going to research many of the same sources as if you were checking to find out if your own civil rights were violated by the dean's office. But for the paper, you're going to have to make sure that you take careful notes; in fact, you'll probably need to copy the sources of your information completely enough that they can be quoted and footnoted. For your own information, you may not need to copy anything beyond perhaps an address and phone number.

Before you research a paper, you must consider who is going to read it. One professor may insist on complete footnotes while another won't require any. One may be partial to hard facts while another prefers original conjecture. A paper that you want to publish may need to include some details that can be left out when you're writing for an instructor who knows you well. A paper that'll be graded by some unknown teaching assistant has to take into account the fact that he may know little about the subject and less about your own brilliant range of background knowledge. Therefore, before you begin any research, pinpoint who it's for: you, a known reader, or one or more unknown readers. Try to get a fix in your mind on how much you can reasonably expect them to know about your topic, and on how much they want to know or expect you to demonstrate that you know about it in the finished paper.

Since most students' major research needs are for course papers, we'll concentrate on that goal throughout this book. Keep in mind that for projects less demanding than research papers, you can often eliminate many of the steps in our shortcuts.

SHORTCUT 2

Make Sure You Know What Your Topic Is

Are you really sure you know exactly what topic you're going to research? Check again. The most common research time-waster—and the biggest one—is not having an exact fix on the topic. For example, researching *cars* can take months and months; researching the *quality of 1972 Fords* will take less than half an hour in a halfway decent reference room. We know of one student who hunted for days in the stacks of the engineering library for information on how computerized exams are put together, thinking that the topic was *computers*. But the topic really was *exams,* and all of the information was easy to find in the education library or in educational references online.

To zero in on an exact topic, check each research subject against two criteria:

1. Do you have *just one* main topic? Let's take the example of the student who wanted to write about computerized exams. *Computers* is one subject, *exams* another. To combine both into one paper, she should have decided on the main topic. As a general rule, grammatical modifiers are subtopics, not main topics. So in writing about computerized (adjective) exams (noun), *exams* is the topic and that's where the research should begin.

Here's another example: Freud and the nineteenth century. If you want to show Freud's influence on the nineteenth century, your main topic is the nineteenth century. But if you're going to research the nineteenth century's influence on Freud, Freud becomes the topic. It's as simple as that.

2. Is your main topic specific enough? Researching *1972 Fords* is a lot more specific than researching the entire subject of *cars*. Just consider how much you *don't* have to read through if your subject can really be narrowed down to *1972 Fords*. Freud, too, becomes an easier research chore if you know that it's just his thinking or his dress that you're interested in or assigned to study.

So narrow down your subject to the most specific aspect that concerns you. Be careful not to make your topic too narrow. *Freud's dress* doesn't include how he styled his beard, for instance, so if you're interested in that, too, what you really want for a topic is *Freud's appearance*. (We've found that few students are too specific in choosing topics; mostly they err on the side of vagueness.)

SHORTCUT 3

Isolate the Purpose of Your Research

Once you've followed Shortcut 2 to the correct topic, you may think you're ready to research it. But don't go tearing off to the library or your computer just yet. Research isn't just finding information. Our dictionary defines it as a search *with a purpose.* If you aren't clear about that purpose before you begin, you'll waste a lot of time aimlessly reading and copying.

The following four purposes encompass almost every specific research project:

1. to find out *how to do something* or *describe how it's done* (whether it's tying a knot or handling your emotions), either for your own information or to offer directions to others
2. to discover what happened at a particular time or place (whether it's history or personal experience or news), perhaps so you can *report* it to others
3. to understand an idea well enough that you can *explain* it to others
4. to find enough evidence so that you're able to *persuade* on behalf of a viewpoint

These four aims should sound familiar. They're also the four different kinds of research papers you're required to write in college: the one that offers directions, the report on events, the explanatory paper, and the persuasive one.

As you move along in school, papers get longer and more complicated. Some may need to fulfill several purposes at once. But one is always the main purpose; all others are secondary. If the major purpose isn't met, the secondary purposes will fail, too. So when you're preparing to research a topic, begin by isolating that main purpose. (See Shortcut 5 for more on isolating your paper's purpose.)

SHORTCUT 4

Keep Your Topic's Time Requirements under Control

Inexperienced researchers often end up drowning in information and wasting valuable time because they've bitten off too big a topic. No matter what the subject, whether it's the universe or the lowly straight pin, you can't research and record *all* of its aspects thoroughly within a reasonable time frame.

How much time is reasonable? We suggest you choose one of the following guidelines.

1. Time-to-grade formula

To arrive at this formula, we began with the following assumptions: (a) Most schools assume that you'll put in two hours' preparation for every hour of class time. (For example, in a five-credit course that meets an hour a day, five days a week for twelve weeks, expect an average of 120 hours of outside preparation time during the semester.) (b) Time spent on a research paper of any length, whether it's 1,000 or 20,000 words long, should be apportioned fifty percent in research, fifty percent in writing and rewriting the paper.

If you work with this formula, limit your research time to the percentage of your grade that the paper is actually worth. For example, a thesis worth five credits all by itself toward graduation may, in your school, be comparable to sixty hours of classroom time, and that should require about 120 outside hours of preparation. Of those 120

8

hours, plan to spend sixty doing research, and another sixty hours doing the writing and rewriting.

If a paper is worth only one-twelfth of the final grade for a three-credit course at the same school, apportion your time this way: 3 (hours a week) × 12 (weeks per semester) × 2 = 72 hours of outside preparation expected for the course; 72 ÷ 12 ($^1/_{12}$ of the grade) = 6 hours you should spend on the paper, 3 for research plus 3 for writing and rewriting.

To find your correct formula, be sure to substitute the numbers that apply in your school.

2. Time-to-length formula

It stands to reason that you shouldn't put in as much time researching a four-page paper as a twenty-pager on the same topic. In fact, you should spend less than one-fifth the time because the introduction and ending for a four-pager will probably run to at least half a page, and the introduction and ending for a twenty-pager in most cases takes up less than one page.

Research time also depends on the kind of paper you're working on. One that's entirely informational needs more underlying researched facts per page than one that's largely opinion. However, we've found that the following formula works for most research. See if it works for you.

- For any paper, allow three hours' initial time to get acquainted with the material;
- For each required page after the first, allow no more than one hour of research time.

For example, a four-page paper should take no more than 3 + 3 (or 6) hours of research. But a twenty-pager might require 3 + 19 (or 22) hours.

These formulas are for classroom research papers and

theses. If the research is for your own needs, only you can estimate whether you're taking too much time. However, once you've had practice researching a few papers correctly, you'll be able to set realistic time limits on all your research projects.

If your chosen topic threatens to loom unmanageable within the research time you've apportioned to it, pare down the topic's scope. You should be able to gauge whether your topic is too broad by the time you've put in your three hours of background work.

One way to pare down the scope is to eliminate some aspects of the topic you've chosen. For example, if you can't cover Freud's *appearance* in a three-page theme, maybe you'd better stick to his *dress;* if you can't cover *the nineteenth century's influence* on Freud, narrow it to *the influence of the political events in nineteenth-century Vienna.* The narrower your topic, the less research time you need to cover it adequately.

Another way to shortcut research time is to eliminate some (or all) of your paper's *secondary purposes.* Just concentrate on the paper's main goal. A twenty-page paper can describe how a video recorder works and persuade the reader that it belongs in every living room. A seven-pager can do one or the other adequately, but probably not both. Remember, it's easier to sound brilliant—and earn a higher grade—if you offer lots of catchy details and several convincing conclusions on a narrow subject, than if you take broad and superficial strokes at a subject that's not narrow enough.

SHORTCUT 5

Pick Out the Correct Working Title

Whether your research is for a paper, an exam, or personal needs, start with a good working title. It's a valuable timesaver. It provides an easy-to-remember record of the topic and purpose of the paper you're researching. If you keep referring to it as you research, it'll keep you from wandering offcourse.

A good working title should do all of the following:

- Show the boundaries of the topic you're researching;
- Include nothing that's off the topic;
- Incorporate your main *purpose* as well as your *topic*.

The wording for your working title needn't be catchy or melodious. It's only for your own benefit, to keep your eye on what you're supposed to be researching. It can be as long and unwieldy as you need. After you've completed your research and written your paper, you can substitute a jazzier title if you like.

Most people do manage to get the right main topic into their working titles. Where they flounder is in forgetting to limit the topic and forgetting to put in the purpose.

By way of example, let's assume you've been assigned to write a five-page essay on Freud and no further limitations have been given. Obviously, covering Freud thoroughly would take a very large book. So the first step is to *limit* the topic. Let's limit it to Freud's dress.

The second step is to show the paper's main *purpose:* to

11

describe, report an event, explain, or persuade. If it's to describe, our working title might be *How Freud dressed for official portraits.* That's limited enough to fit into four pages, or six hours of research time. On the other hand, if the purpose in our above example is to report on an event, we might choose as a working title *How Freud dressed for his own wedding.* If our purpose is to explain something about Freud, we might develop a working title such as *Why Freud dressed the way he did for official portraits.* If our paper is supposed to persuade, our working title might be *Freud's dress for official portraits shows some things about his personality.* We don't yet know *what* Freud's choice in suits, shirts, and socks shows about his ego and id. Once we complete our research, we'll make our final title more specific.

Each of the above working titles severely limits the amount of research you need. Instead of spending your time reading everything about Freud, and coming away with a pile of unrelated facts, you can skip a great deal, pinpointing just the data you need. In half the time, you'll collect twice as much of the wealth of detail that makes graders hand out As.

There will be times when you really don't know enough about some topic to come up with a good working title right at the start. In such a case, put in your three hours of preliminary research, stop, and, before you go any further, decide on your working title.

SHORTCUT 6

Prepare a Preliminary Outline

A good specific working title will help you focus your research energy into the narrowest possible area. To pare down your research time even further, decide exactly what information you need before you set out to find it. The quickest, easiest, and most effective way is to prepare a preliminary outline of the body of the paper you're about to write. (If your research isn't for a paper, you can skip this step and move on to Shortcut 7.)

If you know almost nothing about the topic, you may have to browse awhile before you can work up an outline. But limit this preparatory reading to three hours.

The body of your paper is that long middle section between your introduction and your ending; it reports the details of an event, gives complete directions, thoroughly explains a topic, or argues persuasively for your point of view on the subject. Your outline of the body organizes all these details, directions, explanations, or persuasive arguments into the most logical sequence so that both you and your readers can grasp them with minimum effort.

Once you actually begin to write, you may discover a better sequence for presenting your data. But if you know in advance the general areas for which you need to find facts, figures, authoritative opinions, and such, you can avoid wasting the many hours that poor researchers spend chasing down details that are superfluous or tangential to the paper.

An outline divides your topic into subtopics, and perhaps those subtopics into even more specific sub-subtopics.

In reporting an event, for example, you need a new topic

or subtopic for every shift in time or place. If your paper gives directions, every step that leads the reader toward the goal becomes another subtopic. For an A paper, don't leave out any step, no matter how obvious it seems to you.

For papers that persuade or explain intangible actions or ideas, choosing the right subtopics takes a bit of skill. You've got to *impose* a logical order on the material, such as moving from easy information to hard, or grouping similar thoughts close together. The checklist at the end of this shortcut lists popular ways to organize papers. One of those ways is probably right for your subject.

At first glance, it may seem that one kind of organization works best for part of your paper, and another kind for the rest. However, it's generally best to stick to one organizational pattern—the simplest you can find. Clarity is what wins As on papers, and the simplest, most obvious organization enhances clarity.

The format you use for your outline is up to you. Many people prefer to work with a formal letter-and-number outline:

Working title
  I. Subtopic
    A. Detail
    B. Detail
    C. Detail
      1. Example
      2. Example
      3. Example
    D. Detail
  II. Subtopic
    A. Detail
      1. Example
  (Etc.)

Others prefer simply to jot down words or phrases in the approximate order they're going to be covered. The style you use may change from paper to paper depending on the complexity of the topic and on how much you know about the subject before you begin researching. No matter how you choose to outline, follow these three guidelines:

1. Be sure to write down every subtopic and every important detail on that subtopic that you intend to research.

2. If your paper is about ideas (explanation or persuasion), aim for at least *three* levels of information under each major subtopic. (We did that in the sample outline format above. We'll explain in Shortcut 23 why three is an important number.)

3. Keep your outline flexible. Leave plenty of blank space when you first jot down the outline because you may want to shift around the order or substitute one item for another as you do your research or writing.

In your preliminary outline, you probably won't be able to fill in many of the details or examples. (If you *can,* you probably have very little to research.) Where you don't have the required information, but know that you'll need it, leave blanks or draw lines or put in question marks. It's those empty spots that your research will have to fill in.

To illustrate how outlining can work, we'll reproduce here two actual preliminary outlines we prepared, the first for a 1,000-word article on a topic we knew fairly well before we started, and the second for a 4,000-word article on a very new topic. (We'll refer again to these sample outlines in the next shortcut.)

How to Patch Plaster Walls
1. Preparation for all plaster patching
  a. Tools needed
    1. Spatula or trowel

    2. *Sandpaper*
    3. *??*
  b. Patching products to buy
    1. *Patching plaster*
    2. *Glazol*
    3. *Spackle*
    4. *??*
2. *Patching cracks*
  a. Hairline cracks
    1. *Spread putty with fingers*
    2. *??*
    3. *??*
  b. Deep cracks
    1. *??*
    2. *??*
    3. *??*
  c. Wide cracks
    1. *??*
    2. *??*
    3. *??*
3. *Patching holes*
  a. Small holes (similar to wide cracks)
  b. Large holes
    1. *Cut plasterboard to studs*
    2. *Cut new piece of plasterboard*
    3. *Nail in new plasterboard*
    4. *Feather edges*
      a. Layers of spackle
      b. Feather each layer
      c. Sand
      d. Repaint

Agent X: Biology's "Subatomic Particle"
1. *What is it?*

      a. Chemical composition
      b. Where it's found
      c. What diseases it causes (for sure)
    2. Evidence it exists
      a. Historical
         1. _____
         2. _____
         3. _____
      b. Now
         1. People working on it
         2. Typical experiments
            a. _____
            b. _____
            c. _____
         3. Research techniques being tried
   3. Importance of understanding Agent X
      a. To science & medicine
      b. To mankind
      c. To people researching it
         1. Nobel prizes, etc.

CHECKLIST: POPULAR WAYS TO ORGANIZE PAPERS OR SECTIONS OF PAPERS

GROUP 1. In time sequence:
- in the sequence in which it was seen or done
- in the sequence in which it should be seen or done
- from cause to effect

GROUP 2. From general to specific:
- general topic to subtopics
- theoretical to practical
- generalizations to examples

GROUP 3. From least to most:
- easiest to hardest
- smallest to largest
- worst to best
- weakest to strongest
- least important to most important
- least complicated to most complicated
- least effective to most effective
- least controversial to most controversial

GROUP 4. From most to least:
- most known to least known
- most factual to least factual (fact to opinion)

GROUP 5. Giving both sides (grouped or interspersed):
- pros and cons
- similarities and differences (compare and contrast)
- assets and liabilities
- hard and easy
- bad and good
- effective and ineffective
- weak and strong
- complicated and uncomplicated
- controversial and uncontroversial

SHORTCUT 7

Turn Your Research Needs into Precise Questions

From your preliminary outline, prepare a list of questions. This list is what you'll use as your basic research guide. The questions will keep you on track and zoom you right through the task.

Sometimes there are so few questions, we jot them down right on our preliminary outline; that was the case in the wall-patching example shown in Shortcut 6. Other times we prepare a numbered list; that's how we tackled the Agent X assignment also shown in Shortcut 6. Here's the list of questions coauthor Frank used to research the Agent X story.

1. virus? If so, DNA? RNA?
2. chemical composition?
3. infects? merges with cells? parasite?
4. evolution—what keeps reservoir of Agent X alive?
5. how it causes diseases? kuru? CJD? scrapie? others?
6. discoverer?
7. labs: New York, San Francisco, others?
8. research techniques in use?
9. anybody seen proof it exists? mice? cell culture?
10. importance to science?
11. importance to mankind?
12. Nobel race? other benefits to researchers?

Notice that several hours of preliminary research had given Frank some understanding of the topic. That helped make some of his questions quite specific. For instance, in question 5 he wrote down some of the diseases he already knew were linked to Agent X to serve as a reminder that he had to find out more about these particular diseases. But his question was worded to also remind him that he didn't know all the diseases caused by Agent X. The same goes for question 7, on the laboratories that were investigating this strange infectious particle.

On the other hand, question 6 was quite general. At that point, Frank knew almost nothing about how Agent X had been discovered, and by whom.

It may *seem* like lots of extra work to prepare a comprehensive list of specific questions prior to researching. But the alternative is the kind of research we see all the time: spending hour after hour copying lists of references, half of which are repetitive or beside the point, and then reading piles and piles of material that, while perhaps fascinating, won't be touched on in your final paper.

In the past four years alone, 230 scientific papers, all dealing with the role of viruses in various diseases, were printed in important journals. If Frank hadn't first isolated the specific diseases thought to be caused by Agent X, he would have had to skim all 230 papers just to answer question five. Instead, he read only the twenty or so papers that discussed those diseases, and saved hours of time.

There's another advantage to pausing long enough to work up a list of questions that need researching. For some of your outline subtopics, you may not need to do any research. You may know enough from previous reading, or need just your own opinion or personal experience. With a little thought as you write your questions, you can keep your list down to only the items that you need to research.

Once you've got your questions jotted down, check to make sure that they're the questions you really do need answered. If a question is imprecise or incorrect, the information it helps you collect—no matter how correct and precise it may seem in your notes—might not be the right information for your topic. For your A-quality work, you'll end up with a B on your paper.

SHORTCUT 8

Determine What Kind of Answers You Need

There's another step to take before you begin to research your questions: determine what kind of answers you need.

- Do you need opinion or fact?
- How much authority do you need?
- How up-to-date must your answers be?

For each research question on your list, decide on the answer to these three questions. Then you'll be able to go directly to the right resource materials instead of wasting hours, maybe days, looking in the wrong places.

Here are some guidelines to help you answer each question.

1. Do you need opinion or fact?

Facts come in degrees ranging from *soft* to *hard*. The hardest facts are definitions, numbers, or similar entities with specific, unambiguous meanings to most people. "There are 5,280 feet in a mile" is a hard fact: it's indisputable.

The softest facts are generalizations. They usually accompany qualifiers. Examples are "*most* people like dogs," and "*few* students *really* know how to study." It's difficult to prove or disprove such statements because they're unspecific and so full of qualification.

There's only a fine line between a soft fact and an

outright opinion, and no clear line between hard fact and soft fact. But understanding the differences can often help you get an A instead of a B or C. Some instructors are sticklers for hard facts.

A hard fact must not only be accurate, it must be unquestionably accurate as presented in your final paper. If it's a generally accepted fact—like the number of feet in a mile, or the fact that dogs are popular pets—you may not need to cite a source for your information. The less generally accepted a fact is, the more proof you'll have to offer in your paper. This especially applies to newly discovered facts.

How do you substantiate your facts? By citing some authority that says it's a fact. The greater the esteem of your source, the more believable your fact seems.

In addition to being held in high regard, however, your source should be relatively unbiased. If you quote a health foods magazine to support a statement that large daily doses of yogurt prolong life, the fact is suspect because such magazines are philosophically committed to the opinion that certain foods have life-prolonging properties. If you check out the source of the magazine's fact—the evidence for its statement—and find that it's the result of a careful scientific study, it's better to cite the study for your evidence. But if you find out that the study was conducted by a yogurt manufacturer, you'd better question the credibility of the fact before the person who grades your paper does.

In many cases, one credible, unbiased source for a fact is enough. But when you're working on a paper about something new or controversial, you generally need more than one source for your facts. In fact, being able to cite two sources makes the fact more than twice as credible. If two independent, highly regarded laboratories prove that yogurt prolongs life, it's enough to make most people believe in yogurt.

Therefore, when you're going over your list of research questions, if it's a fact you need, make a note to find (1) a source that's highly regarded and relatively unbiased, and (2) corroboration from at least one more credible source.

Opinion is sometimes much easier to find than fact. Just be sure that your instructor is willing to accept opinions in your paper. Keep in mind that an opinion need not be accurate, nor corroborated from another source. However, you net higher grades if you choose opinions from people with authority.

Opinions are useful when facts are unavailable on a particular subject, and when you need to interpret the facts. But don't make the mistake so many novice researchers do, and waste your time looking for *unbiased opinions*. All opinion is biased by definition.

When you write your paper, make sure you flag opinion as opinion so that a nit-picking grader doesn't think you're trying to palm it off as fact.

2. How much authority do you need?

By now, unless you've spent your formative years in a cocoon, you've learned that there are many levels of authority. The higher a source's level of authority, the more forceful her words seem to be. Consider the statement *"In this school exam grades don't count."* From which of the following sources does it carry the most weight: a teaching assistant, your professor, the head of a department, the dean of students, or the president of the college? No matter whether it's fact or opinion, a statement's impression on the reader grows in direct proportion to the authoritativeness of the source. If a college president says that exam grades don't count, you're going to believe it a lot more than if a t.a. says it.

In researching, you'll encounter two basic types of authority. The first is based on general esteem, and is usually held by people and institutions that have become household names: Ann Landers, Isaac Asimov, the Mayo Clinic, the *New York Times.*

The second type of authority is based on credentials. A Mayo Clinic doctor whose name is not well known takes his authority from the generally known fact that Mayo Clinic doctors are excellent. An unfamiliar researcher whose findings are published in the *New England Journal of Medicine* takes his authority from the reputation of that journal.

Each type of authority has its different levels. Determining these levels is quite subjective. Still, for each question on your research list, you must decide how high a level of authority you need. Authority is like a pyramid: the lower the level, the more authorities you can find. A statement on how to cure teenage acne coming from Ann Landers is less authoritative than a statement made by almost any physician, but for your needs, Ann Landers's observations may be authoritative enough. Information in articles in the popular press (such as newspapers and magazines) is always less authoritative than information from articles in scholarly journals, but for your needs the easier-to-find, popularized information may be acceptable.

If your research is for a course where the relative worth of information sources doesn't count for much, you may want to head for the quickest sources. But if it's a tough course and you want to score brownie points, go out of your way to find impressive sources: the more authoritative the better.

3. How up-to-date must your answer be?

The typical researcher goes to a library, heads for the card catalog, looks up a subject, checks out the available books, and calls it a day. But even a book published only last month is full of old information. By the time a book is written, printed, and tucked away on a library shelf, its contents are at least a year old—generally much more. If the author is a scholar, he probably spent two to five years gathering his research and writing the book.

Some enterprising students also check *Reader's Guide to Periodical Literature* and read up on the subject in current magazines. But even last month's magazine articles were written at least six months ago, on the average. So if you need to know what's happening right now in your subject, you won't find answers there either.

If you want historical information, *Reader's Guide to Periodical Literature* and a card catalog are perfectly fine places to begin. But if you want current facts or opinions, you may have to go right to firsthand sources. (We'll help you find them in Part IV of this book.) Decide, before you start, how up-to-date your answers need to be.

When Frank went down his list of questions for the Agent X story we showed you in Shortcut 7, he found that eleven of them needed the most current answers he could find; his goal was to explain everything that scientists know *today* about the elusive particle called Agent X. The one question that was exempt from this requirement was number six; the discovery of Agent X occurred many years ago. For that one question he could use quick-and-easy sources. For the rest, he didn't waste his time finding out-of-date answers. He looked immediately for timely ones.

SHORTCUT 9

Decide Whether Your Answers Should Come from Secondary or Primary Sources

There are two basic kinds of sources for information. If you get your data secondhand—from someone's report in a newspaper story, a magazine article, a book, or even a movie—you're using a *secondary source*. If you get your information directly from the expert's mouth—or even directly from his own written words—that's a *primary source*.

Primary sources have several advantages:

1. *Reliability.* The expert's own words can be expected to be more precise, and to more accurately reflect his thinking than if they've been sifted through a reporter's typewriter.

2. *Timeliness.* The information you get directly from the source should be his most up-to-date thinking on the subject. What he wrote himself reflects his thinking at the time he wrote it. If you need up-to-date information, you probably need primary sources.

3. *Adaptability.* Secondary sources may not contain precise answers to your particular questions, simply because nobody may have thought to research them before. For such answers, you must go right to primary sources.

Most professional researchers use primary sources to bring their facts and opinions up to date as well as to give them the aura of authority. If you want to create a really impressive paper, find and use as many primary sources as your subject and your research time permit. The extra effort can turn a B paper into one that gets an A.

PART II

PACKING YOUR GEAR: SHORTCUTS THAT MAKE RESEARCH-GATHERING EASY

Most students' research results in a stack of cards, a heap of assorted papers, a sheaf of photocopies, and a pile of books with tagged pages. Before they can begin to think about writing the paper, they've got to organize the material, eliminating what they don't need and putting the rest into some kind of sensible order. Often, the task looms so large, it's put off until just before the deadline. It's no surprise that the result gets a C.

Instead, prepare the right materials so that you can do your organizing *while* you research, right from your list of research questions. It means taking a few minutes extra with each piece of information you find, but it saves hours, even days in the long run, because it makes the at-home organization for your paper as smooth as grease. Procrastination becomes a problem of the past, and the freshness of the material improves your ability to synthesize it.

If you use a different system from ours, and it gets As for you, stick to it. If not, do make the switch.

SHORTCUT 10

Prepare a Work File

Before you compile your first piece of data, prepare a file folder and a looseleaf or spiral-bound notebook, and always keep one inside the other. Paste or staple both your preliminary outline and your list of questions right inside the notebook or folder so they're protected. Also save them in backed up computer files so that if they're lost, you don't lose days attempting to recreate them. Divide your notebook into sections, one section for each question on your list. Tag the sections so you can flip quickly from one to another.

Always keep a left-hand margin of an inch or more on every page of notes. Never write on the left-hand page in your notebook. This will keep your notes confined to one side of the page, and they'll be much easier to rearrange when you're preparing to write your paper. (The same students who cram notes onto both sides of bits and pieces of scrap paper, saving a dollar, are the ones who later spend several dollars in unneeded photocopies.)

Several research guidebooks suggest that you keep your notes on index cards. You can even buy prepackaged cards that have printed title-and-author fill-ins at the top. There are also inexpensive computer programs that make, store, and print these cards. We recommend them only for super-organized people, the kind who never throw a jacket over a chair and have a drawer for everything they own. If you go the card route instead of buying a notebook, purchase the biggest cards you can find so you're not constantly shuffling them in search of the card on which one particular note begins or ends. Then key each card with the number of the question it answers.

Label your file folder with a one-word or two-word project name, and put your name, address, and phone number on it and on your notebook as a safeguard. Into your folder will go all your photocopies and bibliography sheets (a key tool we'll tell you about next). If you work with cards, keep them rubberbanded and invest in a file envelope instead of a file folder to keep the cards safe.

SHORTCUT 11

Keep a Bibliography as You Go

Most college papers call for footnotes or a bibliography. Even for those that don't, you'll raise your grade by citing your sources fully in the text of your paper. To make footnoting a cinch, systematize. Prepare master bibliography sheets, as illustrated here.

Using the illustration as a model, type your own bibliography master sheet on a full-sized (8½″ × 11″) sheet of paper. Photocopy a bunch of blanks, and keep them in your file folder. (To save money, have a large quantity printed cheaply and put them where you'll find them again. Then use them for every research paper throughout school.)

For *each* source in your research, fill in a bibliography sheet, accurately and legibly. Give each in turn a consecutive reference number (the first #1, the second #2, and so on). Keep all the filled-in sheets together in your folder. You can insert the project title (or an abbreviation) before you begin your research. For books, most of the information can be taken right from the card catalog listing. (Shortcut 16 will show how to use the card catalog.)

Do keep a bibliography sheet for each reference you look at, whether or not you use any information from it. For every rejected reference, be sure to fill in a line or two of "comment." *Repeats source X, outdated because . . . ,* and *unintelligible jargon* are all good reasons. There are some sources that a professor automatically expects a researcher to investigate, and you may have to go back after you've turned in your paper and explain why you didn't include that reference.

Fill in a bibliography sheet even if you expect to have the

source (book, periodical, pamphlet, Web site etc.) in your possession when preparing the paper. Having all the information in the same place and in the same format will save time later. For most projects, you won't need to know the price, so we've put that information far down in a corner.

Prepare a Special Source Bibliography sheet (see illustration on page 34) and fill in the applicable blanks for interviews and other primary research (for example, a television interview you've watched). You can make up a number of these sheets, too, in advance; we hope you'll be doing more personal interviews after reading this book.

Why not just fill in all this information for each source in your notes as you go along? For two reasons:

1. With this method, you have all the bibliographic data together, in one set of papers, for footnoting, and can alphabetize easily if you need to prepare a bibliography.

2. By filling in blanks, you'll be sure to take down *all* the information *legibly* right when it's available, saving the hours it takes to hunt down the one page number or correct spelling that you've forgotten to copy in your notes.

Bibliography Master Sheet

Call # _____

Project _____   Reference # _____

Author
Editor _____
         last   first   init.
Title of whole _____
Title of part used _____
(Series title) _____
Second authors
       editors _____
               _____
               _____

Book: Publisher _____

Where published _____

Date _____ (Edition #) _____

Periodical: Volume _____ # _____ Date _____

Web site address _____

Web site sponsor _____ Date accessed _____

Forum name (if an online comment) _____

Total pages of whole work _____

Total pages of part used _____

Comments

Used _____

Not used _____

Special Source Bibliography

Project _____   Reference # _____

Name _____
　　　　　last　　　　　　　　　first　　　　　　　init.

Title _____

Affiliation _____

Address _____

Phone # (   ) _____
　　　　area

Interviewed by _____

Where _____

When _____

Referral came from _____

Related reference information

Re-interviewed? _____
　　　　　　　　　　　　　　dates

Comments

SHORTCUT 12

Key Your Notes for Easy Access

To make footnoting and source-citing easy, we've suggested that you systematize with bibliography master sheets, and that you put a reference number on each sheet. Since each source is fully cited on these sheets, you need never again write down all that information until you get to the final draft, *so long as you key each reference to the appropriate master sheet.*

Some researchers use just the author's last name as a reference key. We also include the master-sheet reference number, as a double-check. When the research is done, we may have two books by the same author or two authors with the same last name. Adding the reference number shows us which is which. (The reference number alone might suffice, except that it's easy to slip and mark two master sheets with the same number. Using both name and number guards against that eventuality.)

There's one more vital number needed to key each piece of information you collect: the page number (or numbers) on which the information appears in the source. If your facts are challenged, it's a snap to support them when you know just where you got them. If you're footnoting, you'll need those precise page numbers for the footnotes.

Your bibliography sheets don't include page numbers, because one source may have many valuable pages of information. You must remember to cite the specific page number of your reference right in your notes. Think *three* and you won't forget: (1) *reference number,* (2) *author's last name,* and (3) *page number.* This three-part key should be used for all the following:

1. *Notebook notes.* For every note you take, write down the key *first,* at the head of the note. (Re-key every new page.) Here's how your notes might look:

> *#5, Jones, pg. 7.* "It's easy to measure your own heartbeat rate." Put right thumb (if r-handed) on l-h wristbone. Keep l-h palm up. *pg. 8.* Now curl r-h index finger around wrist opp. to where thumb is already in position. Adjust the 2 fingers until you feel pulse, "generally just above the wristbone."

2. *Photocopies and computer printouts.* As you photocopy or print, *immediately* write—on each photocopy itself—(1) the reference number, (2) author's last name, and (3) page number of the source of this photocopy. (We circle this key so it's easy to spot.)

3. *At-hand references.* So you won't overlook any reference you expect to copy directly as you write the paper (for example, information in a pamphlet that you've checked out of the library), turn to the applicable section of your notebook and note the essence of the passage. Follow that with the words *see source* and key this note, too, at the beginning with its respective three-part key. Here's how your notebook might look:

> *#5, Jones, pg. 7–8.* Instructions for measuring your pulse to determine heartbeat rate. *See source.*

4. *Interviews.* One interview may answer several research questions. (For help with interviews, see Part IV.) To have the answers where you'll need them when you write the paper, cross-reference your interview notes in the applicable sections of your notebook. To give an example, let's assume that page three of a telephone interview with Dr. Tom Jones contains his instructions for determining heartbeat rate. Here's how the note might look in your section headed *when is exercise harmful?*

#8, Jones interview, p. 3: instruction for how to check
your heartbeat rate.

5. *First draft of the paper.* When you write the paper's
first draft, transfer *each* three-part key in parenthesis or in
the margin right alongside the data it refers to. Then, when
you type the final draft, it's easy to substitute the entire
reference (author, title, and the rest) just by leafing through
the bibliography master sheets.

Your first draft might look like this:

"It's easy to measure your heartbeat rate," says Dr.
(first name) Jones, writing in (#5, Jones, pg. 7). To do
it, if right-handed, put your right thumb on your left-
hand wristbone, keeping your left hand palm up. Now
curl your right-hand index finger around the left wrist
to where your thumb is already positioned. Adjust the
two fingers until you feel your pulse. Dr. Jones tells us
that it's generally found just above the wristbone. (#5,
Jones, pg. 8)

Or it might look like this:

#5, Jones,   "It's easy to measure your heartbeat
pg. 7   rate," says Dr. (?) Jones,
              writing in. . . . To do it, put your
              right thumb (if right-handed) on

Note that we insert question marks, dots, and other
reminders in the first draft, so that we'll remember to copy
the needed data from the bibliography sheets when typing
the final manuscript.

SHORTCUT 13

Take Adequate Notes

As you research, make sure you take adequate notes for each question. In most cases, we suggest you copy the source's own words and, to remind you that they're copied exactly, put quotation marks around them. This saves a lot of backtracking later on.

A rule of thumb is to copy a citation in your own words *only* if:

1. you're absolutely convinced that you'll just use the information, not a direct quotation, *and*

2. there's no possible chance of misconstruing your paraphrase a week later when you've forgotten everything you ever knew about the citation.

If what you're copying is statistical, or composed of other hard fact, it's tempting to just jot down the information in your own shorthand and go on. If you do, make sure you've got *all* the information, not just the bare fact but the provisos and limiters that make it true. To give an example, here's an excerpt from an article published in the *Madison* (Wisconsin) *Capital Times* of September 26, 1977:

City's Serious Crime Up 3%, State Reports

The state's "serious crime index" for Madison jumped three percent in the first six months of 1977, the State Justice Department reported today.

Violent crimes increased five percent, while property crimes jumped three percent.

The Justice Department figures are based on statistics for the first six months of 1977 compared to the first half of 1976.

The largest jump occurred in reported rapes. This year the city has 33 reported rapes, 57% higher than the 21 in the first half of 1976.

No murders were committed, compared to two in the same period a year ago. Robberies were down from 55 to 51, while aggravated assaults dropped from 14 to 13.

The above information seems so straightforward, the average student shortcuts in his notes:

> 1977 vs 1976: serious crime up 3%
> violent up 5%
> property up 3%
> rapes up 57%, 21 to 33
> murders down, 2 to 0
> robberies down, 55 to 51
> aggravated assault down, 14 to 13

But the student intent on an A paper looks for limiters and provisos. Did you catch the following provisos in the newspaper article?

- Just the first half of each year is compared. We have no idea what happened in the second half of the previous year.
- If "violent crime" consists of rapes, murders, and aggravated assaults (the only three possibilities named in the article), two of the three violent crimes *decreased* in frequency, so the bare fact that "violent crime" increased doesn't reflect the whole truth.

The *lack* of provisos in your sources is important to note, too. In this report, neither "serious crime" nor "violent crime" is defined. Does "serious" include "violent"? Does it include property crimes? We have no way of telling. But these are questions we expect a sharp grader to ask if we just report the information as bare fact.

When you take notes, look for qualifying words like *most* and *probably*. Watch for limiting phrases like *of those studied*. Be on the lookout for words that signal opinion, not fact: words like *theory* and phrases like *appear to be*. These limiters and qualifiers can change the meaning and the value of the citation. If you don't want to take the time to do all this important evaluation while you're collecting your research, we urge you to copy the citation exactly, and to copy *everything* that deals with the particular piece of information you intend to use. Then you'll be able to do your sifting while you're preparing to write your first draft.

SHORTCUT 14

Keep Your Notes Legible and Segmented

Most people begin taking notes carefully and legibly. But after an hour of writing, the pen gets hard to hold, handwriting becomes tight and cramped, and abbreviations begin to creep in: *crse* for *course, bl* for *black,* + for *in addition.* A week later, half the scribbles look more like smudges and most of your clever shorthand is impossible to decipher. For *crse,* coarse and crease both make sense; *bl* translates *black* into *blue,* and + looks like a speck of dirt on the paper.

Keeping your notes legible is as important as it is difficult. When you start to scribble, stop a minute and remind yourself of the hours you'll spend backtracking for the right word in payment for the time saved hurrying through now. If you feel a need to loosen your limbs, take a walk to the coffee machine and stretch out those cramped muscles.

You ought to develop a shorthand as you go through school. It will make all note-taking easier, even in the lecture hall. But teach it to yourself slowly, a few words at a time, just as you'd learn a foreign language. If particular words keep coming up in a research project, and you'd like to make up a shorthand for them, jot down a key to your symbols and abbreviations on the first or last page of your notebook just in case they're forgotten by the time you start writing your first draft. (If you prefer to learn someone else's system instead of developing your own, we suggest some of the techniques used in Speedwriting. Look for a book in your library or bookstore.)

If you keep each note in the section of the notebook it belongs in, key each one to its bibliography sheet in the margin at the beginning, and stick to one side of the page; you need not begin each new note on a separate sheet. Simply skipping a line or two between references is enough.

If your words and symbols tend to cramp and squeeze as the day gets longer, make yourself write on every *other* line. It really does keep your letters bigger. In that case, always skip *two* lines between references to separate them at a glance.

If, despite all precaution, you still end up with illegible notes, use a looseleaf book instead of a spiral notebook, or invest in a laptop or palm-sized computer with a good word processing program and a usable keyboard. Some educational libraries have research spaces equipped with computers, but you can't always count on one being available when you show up.

As you research one question, you may come across the answer to another. Using the tabbed book-section method, it's easy to flip to the applicable section of your notebook, key the reference and the page number, and take down all the information you need—and keep from losing track of the question you've been working on. You may find, by the time you get to the last few questions on your list, that you've got more than enough citations to prepare your paper without any further research. (Shortcut 23 discusses how much information to collect for each question.)

Since an interview usually answers a number of questions on your topic at once, we suggest that you take interview notes in a separate part of your notebook. Number the pages of the interview. Leave wide left-hand margins, write on only one side of a page, and key your answers to their respective question numbers in the margins—either right there at the interview or later in your room. Then cross-reference: in the section for each question Jones has answered, write *see interview Jones reference #4, page 2* and then tell, in a few words, the gist of Jones's remarks.

PART III

TRAVELING THE ROAD: SHORTCUTS FOR SELECTING THE RIGHT RESOURCE CENTER

If you've followed all the tips in Part I, you should know just what you're looking for. If you've taken the shortcuts outlined in Part II, you should have your note-taking gear packed and ready to go. Now you've got to figure out where to go. You've got a lot more choices than you realize, and some are better than others for particular projects.

To help you find the right destination, we must first make the distinction between *collected* data and *uncollected* data. *Collected* data is what you'll find in libraries and other resource centers, including Web sites. It consists of recorded primary and secondary information. Uncollected data refers to that huge reservoir of primary information still in the heads of various experts. It's lying there waiting for you to collect it firsthand.

In this section, we'll discuss how to find collected data. In Part IV we'll show how easy it is to tap experts' brains directly.

SHORTCUT 15

Head for the Right Library

The first place to head with your list of research questions is to the right data collector. Most data collections are in libraries. You've probably visited the local public library, your grade school library, and your undergraduate library at college.

For most research projects, your college or university library is the place to start. As a rule, the larger your academic institution, the larger its collection. Many colleges have more than one library, a fact too many students overlook. For example, at the University of Wisconsin in Madison, there are twenty major libraries including an art library, an agriculture library, a pharmacy library, and an astronomy library, as well as a number of smaller, individual departmental libraries such as geology and Afro-American studies.

If your general topic is geology, you'll probably get the best results in the least time if your campus has a geology department library. The information there will be more up-to-date, and it'll be faster to retrieve because it's concentrated in a smaller area than in the vast general campus library that most students head for.

In addition to the public library and your various academic libraries, there are probably lots of other valuable libraries in your town or nearby. One of them may be much better for your particular needs. We'll just touch on a few typical specialized libraries here.

Every newspaper keeps a *morgue,* a library of its past issues clipped and filed on a topic-by-topic, name-by-name basis. Some morgues clip related material from other newspapers and periodicals as well. Most permit researchers to use their files. Many keep their back files online along with a search engine that is fast and easy to use. Some also answer short questions by phone, and respond to mailed requests by photocopying shorter files, usually for a modest fee.

Associations and foundations have libraries too. Large businesses often keep libraries for their researchers and decision-makers. Historical societies and museums stock libraries with valuable collections of specialized materials. The local bar association, the county medical association, the state cancer society, and similar groups all keep libraries of information for their members. Most of these private libraries welcome students. Many keep their back files online for researchers.

You can easily find the location of practically every important library in the country. There are indexes that list most of them. One is the *American Library Directory,* another the *Directory of Special Libraries and Information Centers.* Ask the reference librarian at your school library to help you use one of them.

Once you've located the best library (or libraries) for your purpose, it pays to spend a few minutes learning how it's organized.

SHORTCUT 16

Learn the Library's Book Storage System

Each library has its own book storage system that may be just a little different from every other library's system. Before you begin your first research project at any particular library, learn the way it's set up.

In some libraries, most of the books are kept where only librarians can get to them. To retrieve them, you have to fill out a request card. In other libraries, they're kept on *open stacks.* If the collection is large, the library probably has a printed guide that shows how the stacks are arranged.

To locate books on particular topics, it's quickest to begin your search at the card catalog. To use a large card catalog effectively, you have to understand its filing rules. The rules are *not* identical in all libraries. Are the *Mac*s and *Mc*s filed together or separately? Are they located before all the *M*s, or interspersed? In column A, we alphabetize the entries by grouping the *Mc*s and *Mac*s before the rest of the *M*s. Column B keeps the *Mc*s and *Mac*s in strict alphabetical order. If you don't know the filing arrangement, you could riffle through several drawers before locating McInness.

Column A	*Column B*
McInness	mackerel
MacManus	MacManus
mackerel	Manchester
Manchester	McInness

Is the alphabetization word-by-word or letter-by-letter? This is another subtle but often important distinction between libraries. In one library's system, New York precedes *Newsweek;* in another system, *Newsweek* comes before New York.

In almost all libraries, *author* catalog cards are alphabetized by the author's last name. A book by Henry Ford is found under *Ford, Henry.* But different libraries have different systems for books written or edited by an organization. A book edited by the Henry Ford Historical Association might be filed under *F, Ford (Henry) Historical Association,* or under *H, Henry Ford Historical Association.*

If you use one library repeatedly, it will save you a great deal of time if you learn all the quirks of its filing system. In seldom-used libraries, ask librarians for guidance whenever you're unable to locate material as quickly as you think you should.

Generally, nonfiction books are listed in at least three places in the card catalog: under *author, title,* and one or more *subjects.* (Most fiction is listed under only author and title, and, in some libraries, only under author.) Coauthors, important editors, illustrators, and translators often have "author" cards filed under their names also. If several subjects are discussed fully in a book, it is listed under several subjects. In most libraries, newer books' catalog cards list all the subjects that the book is filed under. In some libraries, only the author entry card for a particular book reveals that information.

A great many libraries file all *subject* cards in one series and *author* and *title* cards interspersed in a second series. Some libraries file three separate series, and others intermingle all three.

A sample *author* card follows on page 48.

PE   Newman, Edwin.
2808   Strictly speaking: will America be the death of
N4   English?   /   Edwin   Newman.—Indianapolis:
        Bobbs-Merrill, 1974
            205 p.; 24 cm.
            Includes index.
            ISBN 0-672-51990-9 : $7.95
1. English language in the United States.   2. Sociolinguistics.   3. United States—Social life and customs.
I. Title

The number at the upper lefthand corner, PE 2808 N4, is
the call number. That's how the book is filed on its shelf.
Since this is an author entry card, the author's name is
added, at the top, to a pre-printed card that's used for all
entry cards: title, subject, author, editor, in some cases even
illustrator. The book's full title comes first in the pre-
printing: *Strictly speaking: will America be the death of
English?* Then comes the author's name. Next is the *city* in
which the book was published (Indianapolis), the publisher's name (Bobbs-Merrill), and the copyright date which is
usually the year of publication as well (in this case it's
1974).

There's additional information, too: *205 p.* shows how
many pages are in the book and *24 cm.* tells its height on
the shelf. Where this card reads *Includes index,* other cards
tell whether the book has a glossary, bibliography, illustrations, charts, photographs, and other extras. The *ISBN*
(International Standard Book Number) is the computerized
identification of the publisher and this book; booksellers
use it to order the book. *$7.95* is its original price, and a
guide to how much you'll have to pay if you check out the
book and lose it.

Finally, the sample catalog card reveals some very helpful
information: the three different subject headings under

which you'll find the book catalogued, *English language in the United States, Sociolinguistics,* and *United States— Social life and customs.* Under each heading, in the subject catalog, is an identical pre-printed card with the chosen subject inserted where the first *author's name* appears on this one.

For most of your research needs, begin with the *subject* of your question (or your topic, if you're starting with preliminary research). For each useful looking book that's card-filed under that subject heading, copy down at least the following information:

- call number
- author's last name and first initial (unless it's a common last name like Jones, in which case you'd better copy down a complete first name)
- title (With long titles, don't copy every word, just enough to help you find the book and remember exactly what it's about until you get your hands on it.)
- copyright date (If you're searching for current information, you can cross off your list all older books if you find enough with very recent copyright dates.)

For books that you're pretty sure you'll be using to find citations, take the time to fill out bibliography sheets from their catalog cards right away. It's a real shortcut.

Once you've found a particularly helpful book, study one of its entry cards to see every subject it's listed under. (For older books, only the *author* entry card has that information.) This may suggest subject headings you haven't thought of yourself.

Another way to locate useful related subject headings, if your library uses the Library of Congress call number system, is to consult the two-volume index *Library of Congress Subject Headings.* A copy is often kept right in the card catalog room. For other classification systems, your library may have comparable indexes; ask.

Many libraries use the Dewey Decimal system of numbers to divide books into categories. Three digits in front of the decimal point classify a book into general categories, and digits after the decimal point classify it into specific sub-categories.

Here's the basic Dewey Decimal system, with some examples of general categories.

000–099   General works (010 = bibliographies; 030 = encyclopedias; 080 = collected works)

100–199   Philosophy (150 = psychology; 160 = logic; 170 = ethics)

200–299   Religion (220 = Bible; 230 = Christian theology; 290 = other religions)

300–399   Social sciences (320 = political science; 370 = education; 390 = customs and folklore)

400–499   Languages (423 = dictionaries)

500–599   Science (510 = math; 530 = physics; 540 = chemistry)

600–699   Applied science and technology (610 = medicine; 620 = engineering; 660 = chemical technology)

700–799   Fine arts and recreation (750 = painting; 780 = music; 790 = recreation and sports)

800–899   Literature (811 = poetry; 812 = drama; 820 = English literature)

900–999   History, geography, biography (910 = travel; 920 = biography; 950 = Asian history)

Fiction is generally shelved separately, alphabetized according to the author's name, even though the Dewey system supplies digits for it. Many libraries also deviate from the system for biographies, denoting them with a *B* followed by a combination of letters and numbers that's keyed to the *subject* of the biography. For example, *B C56* identifies a biography about Sir Winston Churchill. In general, the biographies are arranged *almost* alphabetically according to the subject's name.

The Library of Congress system uses a single letter to indicate broad categories and a second letter for principal subdivisions. Numbers are used for more specific divisions, and decimal numbers and letters add even further subdivisions. As with the Dewey Decimal system, a letter is added that matches the author's last name, and a serial number separates out authors with identical last initials.

Here are some of the Library of Congress system's major categories:

A General works
   AC collections
   AE encyclopedias
   AY yearbooks
   AZ general history
B Philosophy, psychology, religion
   BC logic
   BF psychology
   BP Christianity
   BX special sects
C History: auxiliary studies
   CB civilization
   CS geneology
   CT biography
D History (except the Americas)
   DA Great Britain
   DC France
   DK Russia
   DT Africa
E General history of America
F Local histories of North and South America
G Geography
   GC oceanography
   GN anthropology
   GT manners and customs
   GV sports, amusements, and games
H Social sciences
   HB economic theory
   HD economic history
   HE transportation
   HF commerce
   HG finance
   HQ family, marriage, home
   HT communities, race
   HV social pathology, philanthropy

J   Political science
    JA   general works
    JO   theory of the state
    JX   international law
K   Law
L   Education
    LA   history of education
    LB   theory and practice of teaching
    LC   special forms of education
M   Music
    ML   literature of music
    MT   music instruction and study
N   Fine arts
    NA   architecture
    ND   painting
    NK   industrial arts
P   Language and literature
    PA   classical languages and literatures
    PC   romance languages
    PD   teutonic languages
    PS   American literature
    PZ   fiction and juvenile literature (Many libraries shelve fiction separately, arranged alphabetically by author.)
Q   Science
    QA   math
    QC   physics
    QL   zoology
    QP   physiology
R   Medicine
    RA   hygiene
    RB   pathology
    RE   ophthalmology
    RK   dentistry
    RT   nursing
S   Agriculture
    SB   plant culture
    SD   forestry
    SF   animal culture
    SK   hunting sports
T   Technology
    TA   engineering
    TH   building construction
    TK   electrical engineering
    TN   mineral industries
    TR   photography
U   Military science
V   Naval science
Z   Bibliography and library science

Whichever system your library employs, it puts all books on the same subject near one another. So if your library has open stacks, and you find one particularly helpful book, it pays to browse quickly among books with the same call number to see if you've overlooked any in the card catalog.

Keep in mind that browsing isn't enough. Appropriate material may be buried in books whose *main* topics are completely off your subject. To do a thorough job, use the card catalog and browse.

Some libraries are totally *noncirculating*. They keep all their nonfiction books filed in one sequence. Other libraries have *circulating* collections, too. Most often, their noncirculating volumes are shelved separately, generally in a reference room or on reference shelves. Find out whether your library's reference collection is indexed in the general card catalog or has its own separate index.

SHORTCUT 17

Find the Storage Places for Periodicals

A periodical is a publication that is printed in a series at a set interval. Each publication in the series has the same title. Newspapers, popular magazines, trade journals, and annual reports of businesses, foundations, and other organizations are all periodicals. In large libraries, recent issues are kept on accessible shelves in one room or section, and old issues are stored—bound, microfilmed, or on CD—in another place where retrieval may be by request. Some libraries keep the old, bound issues in the book stacks. Most libraries purchase one copy of each periodical that's likely to be useful to their particular readers, and a researcher's greatest frustration is to discover that the issue she needs is in limbo at the bindery. If that happens to you, see Shortcut 21 for help with interlibrary loan.

The library's reference section has many guides that help retrieve information from periodicals. The one students know best is *Reader's Guide to Periodical Literature*. It indexes only the most popular consumer magazines. For the serious researcher, many periodical indexes are more valuable. Here's just a sampling.

- In the field of medicine, *Index Medicus* is the most complete researchers' guide to periodicals.
- In the field of psychology, *Psychological Abstracts* is the best index to articles.
- In the field of education, *Education Index* is quite complete.

- In the field of economics, *Public Affairs Information Service* (PAIS) *Bulletin* is the guide to go to.
- In the field of modern languages, use *Modern Language Association* (MLA) *International Bibliography*.
- For social sciences and humanities journals, there's *Social Sciences and Humanities Index*.
- For newsworthy information, start with *The New York Times Index*.
- In the fields of practical science and engineering, *Applied Science and Technology Index* is best known.

These indexes are often available, with search engines, on the Internet. Internet searches are much faster than in books, but can miss a lot unless you're very adept at using keywords.

To find authoritative articles and research reports on your topic, it saves time if you begin with the appropriate index and work backward from the most recent applicable entries. From their titles, choose the articles that seem to contain useful information. If you're using a Web site that has hypertext links, a click may take you to the actual article. If not, to find an actual article, you'll have to jot down at least:

- the publication, volume number, and complete issue date (year, month, and, in some cases, even the day of the month)
- the primary author's last name
- the first few words of the title
- the page numbers on which the article appears

For additional tips on using indexes, see Shortcuts 19 and 20.

SHORTCUT 18

Discover Where Pamphlets, Clippings, and Nonprinted Resources Are Stored

Many libraries keep pamphlets, brochures, and even newspaper clippings that they deem especially valuable to researchers. The resources that flop over on bookshelves are often put in file folders, alphabetized according to subject, and stored in *vertical files*—which is a euphemism for file cabinets. These bits and pieces of information are rarely listed in any card catalog.

The Great Neck (New York) Public Library has several drawers full of pamphlets and brochures filed under the general subject heading *Education,* and file-folder subheads include *Scholastic Aptitude Tests* and *Financial Aid.* Other drawers have folders marked *Cancer, Breast-feeding,* and *Teeth.* In the *Teeth* folder, last time we looked, were helpful pamphlets on tooth-brushing techniques and on orthodontics from the American Dental Association, as well as from other groups with vested interests. The library regularly discards old material from its vertical file collection.

Most researchers forget to check the library's vertical files. Many don't even know they exist. But it rarely takes more than a few extra minutes to see if your subject is there.

Another fine source of pamphlets and other short documents is the U.S. Government Printing Office collection. For more about that, see Shortcut 25.

Libraries also store photos, phonograph records, cassettes, films, and filmstrips. Some have old books, pamphlets, and periodicals miniaturized on microform films, microfiche cards, and compact discs so they can be stored compactly in drawers. (To read them, special machines are provided. Don't be too timid to ask for help the first time you use one.) Learn what the library you use most has in the way of these special resources, where they're hidden, and how they're indexed. They will help lead you to a grade-A citation.

SHORTCUT 19

Use the Most Specific Resource Guides First

In the third or fourth grade, teachers introduce students to an encyclopedia for their first research experience. From that time on, students cling to it like a lifeline as they begin every research project.

Unless you need some fast general background in your project, forget encyclopedias. While the information may be correct, and even by-lined by an expert in some instances, sources for specific data are rarely cited and it's difficult to separate verified fact from author's conclusion.

Instead, begin with the most specific reference tool for each question on your list, taking into consideration how up-to-date you need your answer and from how authoritative a source.

1. The most up-to-date and authoritative answers come right from the people who are researching answers to the questions today. Here are some library resources we use to find their names, addresses, and phone numbers.

- *Who's Who and other biographical directories*
    Almost every field of endeavor—science, medicine, psychology, journalism—has its own biographical directory. Addresses and phone numbers are usually included along with achievements. Many reference libraries keep at least small collections of these tools.
- *Journal articles*
    Articles in scholarly or technical journals usually list the institution the author is affiliated with (along with

her name and title) at the beginning or end of the article.

- *Professional and trade associations' directories*

  Executive directors of most associations know which members are experts and which member companies have experts on staff. The directors' names, addresses, and phone numbers are listed in reference guides. (See Shortcut 25 for the name of one guide.)

- *Leads to public relators*

  Manufacturers and sellers of everything from nuts to education, hospital care, and peace are all out to promote their products. The people who do their public relations, while not expert themselves in anything but relating to the public, are often willing to steer you to their resident experts. The library has several guides that help you find public relators. One is listed in Shortcut 25.

- *Leads to federal, state, and local government authorities*

  All levels of government contain informed individuals who feel it's part of their job to inform the public. You can generally locate them by speaking with the Public Information Officer (PIO) of the particular division or department. *The U.S. Government Organization Manual* is an annual guide that lists the PIOs in all the federal offices, along with their addresses and phone numbers. It's available online and at many libraries. PIOs are often happy to send you pamphlets and other documents at no cost.

2. For the most recent data that has been reported, check the index to the appropriate scholarly or technical journals (see Shortcut 17). If the index also *abstracts* a digest or synopsis of the important information in the listed article, it's an even better resource. Often you'll find enough

data in the abstract to tell whether you need to read the article. Sometimes you can even quote facts and figures right from the abstract, and save all the time you'd otherwise spend finding and reading the report. Many journals charge for reading an entire article online but show the abstract for free. *Historical Abstracts, Book Review Digest,* and *Psychological Abstracts* are just three of the many abstracting indexes. Most are online as well as in print, but available only by subscription. Many libraries have subscriptions to the best indexes. Almost any librarian can help you with an online search.

The illustration below shows two sequential listings from *Psychological Abstracts.* Each indexed paper is given a reference number. The first, number 4592, abstracts a paper in the June, 1976, issue of the periodical *Hospital & Community Psychiatry* (volume 27 number 6) on pages 413 through 415. The words *Journal abstract* at the end of the reference tells us that this abstract is taken word-for-word from a summary that appears in the periodical. (Though the summary may have been written by an editor of the publication, it's much more likely that the author wrote it himself.) If your research question is something like, "Are criminals crazy?" you may not need to actually find the article. In your note for that question, you may just have to copy *Petrich, #7, pp. 413–415. Of 434 men and 105 women psychiatrically evaluated (one-third within 24 hrs of booking) by 2 metro jails, almost 50% diagnosed as schizo or manic.* Your bibliography sheet, too, can be filled in right from this entry.

Notice that the next entry, 4593, doesn't abstract the article. Instead you're referred to the abstract in *Dissertation Abstracts International.*

4592. **Petrich, John.** (U Washington Medical School, Seattle) **Psychiatric treatment in jail: An experiment in health-care delivery.** *Hospital & Community Psychiatry,* 1976(Jun), Vol 27(6), 413–415. —Discusses the source of referral, psychiatric diagnosis, and treatment of 434 male and 105 female inmates who were referred for psychiatric treatment in 2 metropolitan jails. Almost one-third of the patients were evaluated within 24 hrs of their being booked into jail. Manifestly disordered and violent behavior accounted for 50% of the referrals; almost half the patients were diagnosed as schizophrenic or manic. The importance of a close working relationship with the custody staff is emphasized as a means of facilitating identification of inmates who need psychiatric treatment. —*Journal abstract.*

4593. **Quinn, James R.** (U South Carolina) **Predicting recidivism and type of crime from the early recollections of prison inmates.** *Dissertation Abstracts International,* 1974(Jul), Vol 35(1-A), 197.*

3. Avoid *Reader's Guide to Periodical Literature* (another favorite of students) for the same reasons you avoid the encyclopedia: Most of the information in popular articles is unattributed and it's hard to separate opinion from fact.

4. If you have a choice when researching historical data, choose *primary sources:* autobiographies and diaries rather than biographies, and original documents rather than reports about them.

5. Learn how to use bibliographies. A bibliography is a list of materials on a given topic. The following are three of the thousands of bound and online bibliographies: *A Bibliography of North American Folklore and Folksongs, A Bibliography of D. H. Lawrence,* and *Bibliography of English Translations from Medieval Sources.* Often, bibliography lists are annotated: that is, they contain comments that help you decide whether a particular item is useful. A complete Walt Whitman bibliography lists all the things he wrote as well

---

*Excerpted from *Psychological Abstracts*

as all the things that have been written about him, in all the most popular languages, along with all the information you need to locate these materials. An even more complete bibliography on Sexual Harassment in America lists not only everything that has been written on the topic in books, articles, and newspapers throughout the world, but all the films and filmstrips that have been produced on the subject. Good academic libraries not only collect thousands of bound bibliographies, but also have bibliographies that have been prepared by doctoral candidates. Collections may be filed in several separate sections. Online bibliographies range from one listing all articles on study and research skills from 1982 on (which we used to update our companion book *Study Smarts*) to a listing, with publication dates, of every book of Edgar Allan Poe's that was ever published.

To find out whether anyone has ever published a bibliography on your topic, you can consult *A World Bibliography of Bibliographies,* the *Bibliography Index,* or a similar volume. Your library may not own the bibliography, but they may be able to borrow it for you through interlibrary loan. (See Shortcut 21.)

Often, the writer of a scholarly book or paper includes a useful brief bibliography of his sources. If so, that fact is usually mentioned on the catalog card or the periodical index listing. Watch for it as you research.

SHORTCUT 20

Skim the Front Matter Before You Use a Reference Guide

We were just looking at the University of Wisconsin-Madison's undergraduate course registration guide. It's full of dots and blips and special symbols that make no sense unless we take a few minutes, first, to skim the front matter. There, we discover that each blip has its own special meaning: everything from "open to freshman" to "an additional hour of lecture each week is to be scheduled by the instructor." You can see that it's important to decipher each blip.

Almost every reference tool you pick up, whether it's a dictionary, an index, a bibliography, or something else, has its own idiosyncratic arrangement and its own special shortcut symbols. In each instance, it's all explained at the beginning of the guide. (If the tool has several volumes, the explanatory text may appear only at the beginning of the first volume.) It really saves time in the long run to take a few minutes to skim the front matter *before* you use a reference so that you understand the arrangement and know where to find the symbols' explanation.

Some guides are produced in triplicate, one alphabetized by author, another by title, and a third by subject. Some intermingle the three. Some abstracts index their works only by number; companion indexes then list these *numbers* under subject, title, and author. (See *Psychological Abstracts* illustration in Shortcut 19 for an example.) Some guides are published and indexed annually, and if you don't know the year of publication of a particular item, you have to search through each year's volume.

Some guides have so many subject headings, they publish companion cross-reference guides to their headings. Many rely on the *Library of Congress Subject Heading Index*. To find all the headings that list information on your particular subject, it's sometimes necessary to consult one of these indexes. To save time, check before you begin using the reference.

Some guides put "*see* . . ." references for alternative subject headings right in the text. For instance, under *Tests* in *Reader's Guide to Periodical Literature* you'll find *see Examinations*. Some indexes vary the *see* references from volume to volume to fit their entries, so watch for that as you research.

When you discover that you need to search several topic headings at once, jot them all down and always search them in the same order. Otherwise, you're bound to overlook a heading here and there as you leaf through the reference tools.

SHORTCUT 21

Make Wise Use of Modern Aids to Research

There's no need to remind you about photocopy machines. They're a standard component of all but the smallest libraries. If anything, students tend to overuse them. It's tempting—and seemingly timesaving—to throw a nickel or dime into the box and have the machine copy the page that contains the quote you may find useful. But then you end up with reams of photocopied pages to sort through. You haven't escaped having to decide whether the material really fits in, whether you need it all, and whether it belongs as a quote or a paraphrase. You've just put off deciding. In many cases, that makes you read and evaluate all the material twice. In addition to wasting money, you really do waste time.

Instead, do your culling right in the library. With your list of annotated questions as a guide, you should be able to decide on the spot whether you need a direct quote, a paraphrase, or merely notes that sum up the information. You should even be able to tell, from the other citations you've collected, whether you need a long quote or a short one.

The same is true of printing out what you find on the Internet. Unless you think you won't find another computer that's connected to a printer later on when you're writing your first draft, just quote, paraphrase, or sum up the reference and its importance and write down its URL (Internet address) so you can find it again.

We don't photocopy or print out a page unless we're planning to quote directly more than four or five lines from it. When we do photocopy or make a printout, we circle the applicable part immediately so we don't have to read the entire page again.

Remember to key the page to your bibliography sheet by writing the author's last name and reference number on it, and make sure to add the number of the question it answers.

The Internet is filled with up-to-date and historic information about everything under the sun, much of it free for the taking. But to find it, you have to choose a good search engine for your needs, learn how to use its search rules and shortcuts, and get very good at choosing the right *keywords.*

Search engines keep complete, up-to-date information about nearly everything on the Web. Some are more family oriented than others and favorites keep getting replaced by newer, better favorites. We used AltaVista until Google came along. Some services are useful for special searches even when they're not best for everything. For instance, Lycos, unlike Google, lets you specify whether to find what you're looking for in text on the site or in the site's name (URL).

Most search engines provide their own list of search rules and shortcuts, though some make you search their site hard to find them. Since not all services mean the same thing by word strings, or use the plus symbol or quotes around words the same way, it pays to read your favorite site's tips before starting your first serious search. It also pays to click on and use *Advanced Search* when available.

Most important, however, is choosing the right keywords to search. (Google's internal list of synonyms makes the job a bit easier.) When we looked up *search* + *"key word"* in Google, it found 753,000 hits (Web site pages where the two appeared together). When we changed it to *"search engine"* + *"key words"* + *"Web search"* + *tips* and used Advanced Search to request pages updated in the last three months, it narrowed the results to about 650 hits, a number we could reasonably scan in a few minutes. (It helps if you opt to see 50 results on a page rather than 10.) If the engine is good, you'll usually find what you need within the first 50 or 100 results.

Guard against narrowing your choices so much that you block out half of what you're looking for. This is particularly true if you're using a Web site's own search engine. When we searched eBay for auctions of the Braun Oral-B Excel Model D17535 electric toothbrush, we missed seeing half the auctions until we just searched on Oral-B Excel.

If you need more help learning how to use keywords and search rules, you can find it by typing *"search engine"* + *"key words"* + *"Web search"* + *tips* as keywords in your favorite search engine.

When you're researching in a library, don't overlook the excellent online research services, such as Dialog and Nexus/Lexus, to which many libraries subscribe. You can usually search them from the library for free or for a very low cost. Also learn to use *interlibrary loan.* If your library doesn't have a book, periodical, CD, or other reference tool that you need, it can often be borrowed from another library in the United States or Canada through a reciprocal lending network. In addition, the Center for Research Libraries lends its book and periodical collection to academic libraries and sells reprints of articles at nominal cost. The United States Library of Congress, too, circulates part of its collection to serious researchers through interlibrary loan, but you may have to hunt to find a librarian who knows how to use the service.

You can't depend on interlibrary loan for last-minute research, since requests often take three or four weeks to fill. But it pays to become familiar with the interlibrary loan apparatus at your library and to make interlibrary loan one of your first research priorities whenever you've got a long-term project that may call for borrowed materials. If you have a hunch that some vital source or citation is unavailable locally, spend your first few research hours checking on that material and filling out interlibrary loan request slips.

SHORTCUT 22

Ask the Librarian

If your waterpipes spring a leak and you know little about waterpipes, you don't dab here and tinker there; if you're smart, you call a plumber. If a cut won't heal, you don't try this remedy and that for very long; you see a doctor. Yet students wander through stacks and stacks of books, periodicals, card files, indexes, and the like—sometimes for days—trying to find the repository of an elusive bit of information, when an expert is waiting, free for the asking, to point them to what they need.

Librarians are experts in finding hidden information. They've had several years' training and some experience on the job. A really good librarian, like a good doctor or plumber, is a miracle worker. He can find quick answers to questions that seem insoluble. What's more, it's his job—it's what he gets paid for. So learn the names of the best librarians at the libraries you frequent, and learn when they're on the job. Use their services wisely; don't expect them to do your research for you. But do go right to them when you've got a specific question and you don't know where to start seeking an answer. The more specific the question, the quicker you'll be pointed in the right direction.

If a librarian goes off to look up an answer for you, always tag along. For one thing, you need to copy the specific bibliographic data; for another, you need to verify the information for yourself. Most important, the reference that has one answer may have answers to more of your questions; so always read not just the part your librarian points to, but the surrounding information as well.

SHORTCUT 23

Research to Fit the Rule of Three

Three is a magic number. Make a general statement and offer three specific proofs to back it up, and you can convince almost anyone that it's absolute gospel.

Professional nonfiction writers use this rule of three all the time. For every conclusion, they offer three specifics. An authoritative quotation (or a paraphrased quote) is one kind of specific. Another is a true-to-life *anecdote,* or little narrative, that illustrates the point. A fact, coupled with mention of its authoritative source, is a third kind of proof. You can mix and match any of these specifics together to make your point, but to score a top grade you should aim for *three.*

When we collect data, we try to find *at least* three separate specific answers for each question on the list. We aim for several extra answers, so that we can choose the best or liveliest three when we're writing. For instance, to answer Frank's question 7, *labs: New York, San Francisco, others?* (see Shortcut 7), he found reports of findings from numerous laboratories including one in Albany, New York; another in Montana; a third in Bethesda, Maryland; and several in Japan and Paris, France. To gather direct quotations and anecdotes, he telephoned Bethesda, Albany, and San Francisco, and never had to mention Montana, Paris, and Japan in his article.

Once we've found enough specifics to select from (or convince ourselves that only one or two answers exist) we stop researching that question and go on to the next one on the list. Knowing when to stop is easy when you keep in mind the rule of three.

SHORTCUT 24

Stick to Dependable Sources

It saves time and raises grades to stick to dependable sources and to keep conscientious track of who they are, no matter how brief or obvious the information is. There are two practical reasons.

1. It makes your paper weightier

Consider the following statements from three different papers. Which one makes the greatest impact?

- There won't be any drinking water left ten years from now.
- A *Mother Earth News* article states that there won't be any drinking water left ten years from now.
- Dr. John Jones, Professor of Limnology at Harvard University, is quoted in *Mother Earth News* (December, 1982) as saying that there won't be any drinking water left ten years from now.

The more dependable your source, the more important it is to refer to it in your paper. A paper filled with careful, complete mention of dependable sources gets an A.

2. It takes you off the hook

If you say there won't be any drinking water left ten years from now, without attributing the information to anyone else, you must personally stand behind the statement's accuracy, like it or not. If, instead, you include the source of your data, you are reporting it. Aside from sounding more authoritative, it also leaves you practically in the clear if somebody else got her facts wrong.

The more dependable the source of the data, the more likely the facts are to be correct. *Fortune* magazine employs people just to check the facts in its articles before they're printed; many smaller business publications do not. *The Wall Street Journal* is carefully proofread for errors before publication; *The New York Times* no longer is. Many scholarly journals ask the authors of their articles to correct errors in the galleys (the words set in printer's type) before publication; most consumer magazines do not. If you're building a case on the quotation, "There won't be any drinking water left ten years from now," you must consider the reliability of the source. Your entire paper could collapse if ten is a typographical error and another student cites a more dependable source for the figure *100*.

SHORTCUT 25
Skim for Your Answers

Most students read too much when they're doing research. Resist the temptation. There's no need to read every word. Learn how to skim for answers. It's easy if you research your questions one at a time.

Keep the question in mind as you skim. You may find, at first, that you have to keep rereading it to remind yourself. After awhile, you'll get the hang of it. Then force your eyes to sweep whole pages at a glance, looking for clue words that flag the answer. For example, in answering question 6 (Shortcut 7), *discoverer?* Frank skimmed the likely literature just looking for variations and synonyms of that one word (leader in the field, father of, chief investigator).

Before you even begin to skim pages, use whatever shortcuts the reference work provides. The table of contents may be detailed enough to limit your skimming to small portions of the book. The index may list the clue word, confining your skimming to just those references. The work may be abstracted at the beginning or summarized at the end. Check beginning and end before you skim. There may be convenient topical signposts scattered through the work. The arrangement of subject matter may lead you to the specific portion you need to skim, and permit you to skip the rest.

It may seem counterproductive to suggest that you answer just one question at a time. But it really does save time in the long run. That's because most people can't skim successfully for more than one topic at a time.

But often, in skimming, your eye lights on the answer to one of your other questions, and you recognize it. In that case, do stop and flip to the appropriate place in your notebook, and make all the notes you need. Then head right back to the question you'd been working on.

Don't permit yourself to slip off the paper's topic, onto a tangent, no matter how fascinating it is. If it's something you really want to read in detail or track down in greater depth, make a quick note of it in some *other* notebook and forget it until another day. Half the fun of researching is stumbling onto intriguing facts and ideas that suggest new avenues for future exploration. But don't let one of these tangents sidetrack you or slow you down now.

SHORTCUT 26

Find Leads to Literature from Groups with Causes

Back in fourth grade coauthor Judi had a teacher who was savvy when it came to research techniques. She knew that countless organizations sent out reams of helpful fact sheets, pamphlets, and brochures for just the cost of a postage stamp. The heavy packages of colorful materials that arrived from foreign consulates not only whiled away rainy days and led to several years' worth of grade-A social studies reports, but provided a lesson so graphic Judi never forgot it.

Since then, the cost of a request letter has increased sevenfold, but the return on your investment is still great. Any group with a cause—whether it's promoting tourism, combatting heart disease, selling instant cereal, or keeping a congressional representative in office—grinds out literature that not only promotes its cause, but includes useful facts, figures, research reports, photos, and charts, much of it free for the asking, or, even better, by just searching the group's Web site. Many groups produce reams of technical information for serious researchers in addition to their simplified reports for the lay public.

Your library has good guides to the names and addresses of these organizations. There are directories of manufacturers (like *Thomas Register of American Manufacturers*), of professional and trade associations (like *The Encyclopedia of Associations*), and of nonprofit organizations (like *The Foundation Directory*). A number are arranged by subject so that if you want information on spark plugs or heart disease, you can find listings under the appropriate heading.

For quotable facts and figures, there is no library (except the Library of Congress) that contains as much up-to-date, often practical data as the huge library of publications ground out by the U.S. Government Printing Office. Every state in the U.S. has one or more designated libraries that are required to store every one of the publications in pamphlet or CD form. Many are also available online. Most campus libraries subscribe to the *U.S. Government Publications Monthly Catalog* for their reference collections, and once a year the catalog contains a full-year index to subject matter. In addition, there are bibliographies of past government documents going all the way back to 1774.

All levels of government, from towns to international organizations like the United Nations, issue statistical publications, legislative records, and technical reports, online or in print. Many are important *primary* research sources. Your library may have some; others may be located using special indexes and then obtained directly from the publisher. In some cases, your local government representative may be able to get you a publication that's unavailable by any other means. (When asking a legislator for help, do mention the fact that he's your representative.) If you're stymied, take your question to that good librarian we discussed in Shortcut 22.

When you use any data provided by organizations eager to promote products, causes, or particular points of view, you must always carefully evaluate the credibility of the information and, if possible, verify its accuracy using a second source.

PART IV

GETTING INTO UNEXPLORED TERRITORY: SHORTCUTS THAT REACH THE EXPERTS

Most students—and many instructors—assume that a research paper can only be researched in a library or online. But that isn't true. Professional writers know that the best and most up-to-date facts and opinions haven't been published yet. To spark their articles with the fire of a new observation or conclusion, they head for the experts who are at work on the subject right now.

To be guaranteed a higher grade than your classmates, shake up your instructor. Include some information that's never been published. Seek out a few experts.

SHORTCUT 27

Write Letters That Get Your Questions Answered

The first choice of students, when it comes to reaching a real live expert, is to send a letter requesting the information that's needed. We consider it the poorest method of attack unless you need just a few short answers, and unless your questions are both simple and so precise that there's no chance to misconstrue them.

Even with these provisos, there are eight steps to successful research by mail. (A sample letter is illustrated on pages 84–85.)

1. *Address your letter to a real person* (Mr. John Jones, Director of Research), *not simply to a title* (Director of Research). Otherwise, your letter will probably be read—and answered—by an anonymous secretary or intern. If John Jones reads and answers it, he knows that he must assume responsibility for the accuracy of his response. Not so for Secretary X.

2. *Tell why you need the information.* A serious researcher preparing a thesis or planning a course of action gets a more careful response than someone who's just curious.

3. *Tell why you need his help.* Explain why his particular expertise is needed. It not only makes your request seem less frivolous, but may flatter him into a longer or quicker response.

4. *Tell how the information is to be used.* Is it for a class assignment or to help you make a personal decision? Are you asking for permission to quote the person? Do you expect to publish the answer? If so, will it appear in the school newspaper or a scholarly journal? You can't quote a person in print unless you tell her in advance.

5. *Ask specific questions.* If there's more than one, number them so the responder can just jot down abbreviated answers. Leave room in the margins of your letter for handwritten answers. A busy executive may keep a letter for weeks if she has to dictate a response to her secretary, but if she can just scribble quick answers, she may decide to do it right then and there. (The illustration shows an actual request letter and its response.) Phrase your questions so they can be answered briefly, and don't expect more than a few words for each response—though you may be pleasantly surprised.

6. *Refer to your deadline.* If you don't have one, create one: it helps people respond quicker. If there is no deadline, the letter tends to get buried and even lost. But do give a realistic deadline. Take into account the time it takes the Postal Service to get mail from here to there and back, and in addition allow at least a week for the expert to frame her reply.

7. *Have your letter typed; keep it businesslike and short—no more than one page long.* Busy people put aside lengthy letters. (To hone your letter-writing skills, we recommend Chapter 13 of our college textbook *Good Writing*.)

8. *Enclose a stamped, self-addressed envelope—even if the expert's at a million-dollar corporation.* That's to encourage her to slip her scribbled reply right into the outgoing mail.

9. Include your e-mail address and suggest that you'd be happy to get a response by e-mail if that's easiest. (But never e-mail a source who hasn't e-mailed you first and said it's ok to e-mail back. It's very impolite unless you're sure the source wants e-mail.)

SAMPLE OF RESEARCH BY MAIL
(address & date)

(salutation)
Dear Mr. P_____,

I am under contract to M. Evans Publishers to write, for 1975 publication, a full-length guidance book for undergraduate students who are considering a temporary drop-out from school. One of the questions I'd like to answer is, "When you apply to medical school, will the fact that you dropped out of college for a while affect your application?"

I have chosen your medical school as one of several from which to solicit guidance. I'd appreciate it if you, or an appropriate colleague, would take a few minutes to answer the following:

1. Does your medical admissions committee have a policy for or against "stop-outs"—temporary dropouts?
2. Is a leave of absence considered more respectable than a drop-out or transfer to another college?
3. Is it better for an applicant to have dropped back into the college he left, rather than another one?
4. Is it better to have stopped out during college or after high school?

As a result of my research, I hope to be able to give realistic guidelines for students who are bright, thoughtful, and groping for identity—and yet hoping to go into medicine some day.

I enclose a stamped, self-addressed envelope. If you prefer, e-mail your answers to me at [e-mail address]. Because of an early manuscript deadline, I'd appreciate a response by December 15.

Sincerely,

(signature)

Judi Kesselman-Turkel

Here's the response this letter got from one source.

Judi—

The Admissions Committee has no policy for or against "stop-outs." It is my opinion that they are not at a disadvantage. I further believe it is better to stop-out than collect bad grades that will never be competitive. (These are my opinions.)

Jim P——

SHORTCUT 28

Make Face-to-Face Interviews Pay Off

When we want an expert for our articles on anything from the weather to tomato canning, we head first for the local university. Yet few students take advantage of the resident experts right on their own campuses. If you're engaged in serious research, most professors are pleased to take the time to talk to you.

But don't just go barging into the Meteorology Office or the Ag Science building and corral the first instructor you see. Instead, approach interviewing the way the pros do. You'll get a great deal more useful information in the same length of time.

1. *Define for yourself the reason you need the interview.* If you don't do that before you begin, you'll end up with a conversation, not an interview.

2. *Let the expert know your purpose in advance.* Set up an appointment. Ask for enough time. (Usually up to a half hour is easily given.) Let the expert have at least a day's notice to think about the topic. She may even find a helpful paper or prepare a useful chart.

3. *Write down a list of questions that the expert can answer for you.* But use it as a guide, not a bible. Make sure you get all your questions answered, but be prepared to ask other questions that are suggested in the course of the interview. Keep your questions simple, and ask them one at a time. Complex, multifaceted questions often get partial responses. Most people think and speak one thought at a time.

4. *Know something about the topic and the expert before the interview.* Do some background research so your questions show intelligence instead of ignorance. You'll get more thoughtful answers.

Know the expert's title and the spelling of her name. (You can get it from a secretary.) If she's written books or papers on the subject, skim them before you see her so that you don't ask questions she's answered in print. Do ask for clarification of what you've read, if you need it. She'll be pleased to see that you've done your homework.

If the topic is technical, become familiar with the field's vocabulary before the interview, so that you can follow the expert's words without having to keep asking their meaning. (If you're prepared, and still a strange term is used, do ask its meaning.)

5. *Get off to a good beginning.* Get to the interview on time. (If you're late, it's your time you've wasted, not hers.) Take several pens in case one fails, and take notes in your project notebook, not on scraps of paper. Avoid using tape recorders. There are too many problems that can come up—not only with the machinery (run-down batteries, no convenient electrical outlet, poor volume control, etc.), but also with your interviewing style. If you take notes instead of fooling with a tape recorder, you will remain more attentive and remember things more clearly. In the long run, you will save time, too. Do you really want to listen to the interview again? And transcribe it all?

Get right to the point of the interview: remember, you're not there for a social visit. If there's time left at the end, you can chat then. (If the prof likes chit-chat, you may have to come right out and say that you'd prefer to get your questions out of the way to be sure there's time for all of them.)

6. *Listen to the answers you get.* Make sure you understand them. If you're not sure, double-check by asking,

"Did you mean . . . ?" Often, answers suggest new questions. Too many interviewers are so busy taking down answers, they don't follow through with those questions. Use the shorthand you use in lecture note-taking. You don't need entire sentences unless you're planning to quote the person, and even then she won't expect you to get her precise *words* down, only her precise *meaning*.

7. *Keep your comments to a minimum.* The expert can't give information when *your* voice is in gear. Self-evident as it is, this fact is overlooked by many interviewers. They monopolize the interview with their own inexpert opinions.

On many occasions, we've actually used silence as an interview technique. We've waited after an answer as if to suggest, "Is that all you have to say?" Often, we've been rewarded with more elaboration: a good example, a spontaneous evaluation of the fact, or a restatement that's much clearer than the original remark.

8. *End with an open-ended question.* "Is there something I should have asked that I didn't?" is sometimes the most useful question in the entire interview.

9. *Ask for referral to other experts on the subject.* Your interviewee often knows who's doing the most up-to-date and important research in her field. She'll be happy to tell you who to contact. When you do, it'll grease the wheels when you say, "Professor X suggested I speak with you."

10. *Leave as cordially as you came.* Don't linger after the time that's been allotted to you—though if the expert volunteers more time, accept it graciously if you need it. Ask, as you leave, if you can get in touch again in case you've missed a few important points or need clarification of points already made. Other questions might occur as you do more research.

These ten steps will lead to a grade-A interview, whether it's with the local homecoming queen or the president of General Motors.

SHORTCUT 29

Use the Telephone or E-mail

Most people go out of their way to avoid telephoning strangers. For some odd reason, the fear of a slammed receiver is greater than the fear of a slammed door. If you approach telephone interviewing as professionally as we suggested you attack face-to-face meetings, you need have no fear.

Even when the expert is a short walk away, we often prefer telephone interviews. Busy people who can't schedule a half hour in the office until several weeks hence, often squeeze in the time much sooner for ten minutes on the phone. In a ten-minute phone call, we usually get as much information as in a half hour sitting with the person, and we also save the time it takes to travel back and forth.

1. *If you want to reach a particular expert, or speak for more than a minute or two, write or phone the secretary in advance and suggest a telephone appointment time.* Explain what you're after and why, just the way you do when setting up a face-to-face interview. Then be sure to remember to phone again at the arranged time.

2. *Use the good interview techniques described in Shortcut 27.* But don't take notes. The silences while you transcribe eat up too much telephone time. Instead buy a telephone pickup for your cassette recorder or use your phone's built-in digital recorder if it has one. It's legal to record from the phone so long as one of the two speakers agrees to it; since you're one of them, you're on perfectly legal grounds. (You may want to tell the other person that you're recording, to insure that he'll speak at his normal rate of speed.) While the interview is still fresh in your mind, be sure to transcribe the tape or take the notes you need from it. Poor pickup due to unforeseen noises may blur some answers, and weeks later you won't be able to fill them in from memory.

Many experts provide their e-mail addresses online. Some specifially warn against e-mailing by students looking for easy homework answers, but others invite serious researchers to e-mail them with questions. If your expert invites e-mail, make sure that your e-mail doesn't look like spam. On the subject line, put "Request for Clarification of Your Research" and avoid starting the e-mail with, "I am a student . . ." Instead, start right in by quoting what the expert said or wrote, tell where you saw it, and ask your question or questions about it. To look like a serious researcher, make sure your tone, spelling, grammar, and punctuation are faultless. And keep your e-mail short.

SHORTCUT 30

Become Your Own Expert

For some questions on your list, it's conceivable that nobody's yet found the answers. You may have to compile your own data. Coauthor Judi ran into that problem when she was researching for her book *Stopping Out*. She could discover no document that answered the question, "Do medical and law school admission committees penalize students who've stopped out?" and no expert who'd studied it either. So she prepared her own *survey* of individual experts. She sent the question (in the letter format shown in Shortcut 26) to the chairmen of twenty-eight selected medical school admission committees and nineteen law school admission committees. She received replies from sixty-three percent of the law schools and thirty-eight percent of the medical schools—enough, it turned out, to enable her to make valuable generalizations for readers. On this topic, she became her own best primary resource.

Often, papers for science, social science, and education courses are based almost entirely on primary research: a laboratory experiment, a set of field observations, a survey or opinion poll, or a combination of several techniques. These papers must put the author's original research into the perspective of what's gone before, so do remember to research that data before you begin your own investigation.

Unless you've had some good courses in statistical methods, *your* idea of a survey and your *professor's* may be miles apart. He may expect you to be familiar with such terms as *chi square, null hypothesis, matrix,* and *confidence level.* If they sound like Greek to you, the best course is to discuss your projected survey with the instructor. An *informal survey,* carefully labeled just that, may be the best way to fill a blank spot in your paper.

PART V

ROADMAP FOR A GRADE-A PAPER: USING YOUR RESEARCH MATERIALS

If you've followed the routes we've plotted for you, you should have, by now, (1) an outline for a paper and (2) the research facts and citations you need to plug all the holes in the outline. Now comes the hardest part: putting the two together. What follows is a step-by-step guide to getting from here to there.

SHORTCUT 31

Rethink Before You Write

When you've completed all your research, collect your file of photocopies, printouts, and bibliography sheets, the at-home books and clippings that you'll be copying from, and your notebook of answered questions. In your notebook, safe from harm, is the tentative outline you made at the beginning of the project. Now it's time to reevaluate the outline, so pull it out and begin.

1. *Does your working title still completely reflect both your specific topic and your approach?*

If you haven't found much about Freud's clothing, but found a lot about the cut of his beard and the style of his hairdo, you might want to narrow "How Freud's Appearance . . ." to "How Freud's Facial Appearance . . ." If you uncovered the surprising fact that several Parisians influenced his appearance more than nineteenth-century Berlin did, you'll need to shift your title "How Nineteenth-Century Berlin Influenced . . ." to "How Three Nineteenth-Century Parisians Influenced . . ." Now's the time to zero in on your final working title for the paper. Make your changes right there on your outline.

2. *Does your outline still seem to deal with the topic in its most logical order?*

Review the checklist in Shortcut 6, if necessary, to find a better progression of subtopics. Make your revisions to the outline.

3. *Have you found any new subtopics that must be included to make your paper complete?* Put them where they belong.

If you've made more than two or three revisions, it's best to update your outline at this point.

4. *If you haven't already done so, give each topic, subtopic, sub-subtopic, and so on a letter or number.* (The formal I, IA, IB, II, III outline shown in Shortcut 6 is a good one, but you can use any system you like.) This step is extremely important.

5. *Now go through your notebook and, in the margin in front of each separate note, write the number or letter in your outline into which this particular piece of research fits.* We use a pen of a different color from the one we used to take notes and circle the key number so it stands out when we skim through later on.

Because your questions have been prepared from your tentative outline, most of the answers to a particular question will receive the same key number. But because you may have changed your approach slightly, or revised your outline a bit, some sources for one topic may now be in with another topic. So think as you key; don't let it become an automatic procedure.

6. *Check your key numbers against the outline to make certain that you have at least three supports for each generalization.* If you don't, you have two choices: either complete your research before you begin your first draft, or—if there's just a small hole or two—write the draft if you like, and then fill in what's missing. But remember, if it's a grade-A paper you're after, don't get lazy about filling that hole or two.

7. *Finally, take all your pages of notes (except interview notes) out of your notebook, pulling carefully if you've been using a spiral notebook.* Cut them apart on those skipped lines between references. Then reassemble them according to key number and paperclip or staple all the references for each key. Put them in order, and keep them in your file folder so they don't get lost. When you write your first draft, simply pull out each set of research notes as you get to it. This method often cuts out hours of flipping back and forth to find the right reference, and practically insures that you won't overlook any of them.

SHORTCUT 32

Zip Through Your First Draft

Students who choose meaty topics, research brilliantly, and take enviable notes, sometimes get totally hung up on the simple task of beginning a paper. They ponder for hours, days, weeks, in front of that first blank page, wondering how to start.

Here's a tip to cure writer's block before you catch it: start your paper by plunging in. If, after fifteen minutes of thought, you can't think of a better way, begin with that old grade-school standby, "In this paper I am going to tell about . . . The reason I chose this topic is that . . ." Once under sail, the impetus will keep you going. When the paper's all written, it's a great deal easier to find the best first paragraph.

That's because, once you're past the introduction, you're into the body of the paper—and the body is nearly completed. All you do, when you write it, is drape your outlined generalizations with the specifics that are there in your notes, and put it all into complete sentences.

Write with thought and attention to your ideas, but not to the mechanics of spelling, punctuation, or grammar. At this stage, simply get it said—with as few starts and stops as possible. Don't hunt for the right word, either. If you feel you need reminders, you can type question marks near words that you'd like to improve on. In this draft, the emphasis should be on putting all your material on paper as logically and quickly as you can. Mull over ideas, not their best execution on paper. When you edit this draft, before you print your final paper, you can put spit and polish on your prose.

Don't bother to type precise, detailed references to your sources or bother with footnotes. Instead, key your manuscript to your citations using the *author's last name, bibliography reference number,* and *page number* information that heads up each reference. We sometimes put that data in parentheses right after what we're quoting or paraphrasing; sometimes we add it parenthetically at the end of the passage that relies on that research note. When we edit the draft, it's easy to substitute footnotes or end notes, when needed, right from our bibliography sheets.

Even when there's no footnoting requirement, it's good to have these reference numbers right there in the first draft. We print the draft and save it in the folder for the project, and if a researcher at our publisher's office asks where we got our information, we can promptly cite the source right down to the page number. If an instructor questions your data, she'll be impressed if you, too, come up with a prompt, complete citation.

We recommend that you type your first draft in a good word processing program. Some writers do well writing longhand, but we've found that students who learn to think of words at the computer learn to write well faster because they see a full page at a glance and change it fast if it's not what they meant to say.

When you're done, print out the draft and edit it on the printed pages, where you can more easily move back and forth. If you type (or pen) your first draft double-spaced or even triple-spaced, you'll have room between the lines to make revisions. If you leave wide margins (a professional inch-and-a-half at the left and an inch each at the right side, top, and bottom) you'll be able to use the margins to insert notes to yourself and corrections that don't fit between the lines. (The page or two you save now by writing edge to edge will be lost later when you have to print again due to confusing insertions.)

If you come to a subtopic that needs the weight of more specific information than you have, *don't stop;* just add a reminder in bold type, put it in parentheses, and go on. If you keep up the momentum as you are writing, your paper will be much more cohesive than if it's done in stops and starts. For the same reason, if you suddenly think of a new argument or discussion topic as you write the first draft, put it down now in as much detail as you need to remember it, and leave space for supporting evidence. If one of your notes is garbled or missing an important detail, correct that, too, after you've finished this draft.

SHORTCUT 33

Choose the Best Specifics in Your File

Way back in Shortcut 23, we suggested that you collect a little more research than you need. That little bit extra will come in handy now, as you write your first draft. For each statement, you can pick and choose the best three pieces of evidence in your file. For each scene, you can isolate the best three details. For each argument, you can cull the best three supports.

Depending on the purpose of your paper, and also on the preferences of the person who's going to grade it, your choice of "the best" can be made in one of two ways.

A. Sometimes the best piece of research is the one that's the most *interesting*. Anecdotes, for example, are usually more interesting to read than dry facts.

Long years of writing for a wide variety of readers have taught us to trust our instincts when it comes to judging whether something will interest our readers. If it interests us, it almost invariably interests them. So be sure to include in your paper the discoveries that intrigued you.

B. Sometimes the best piece of research is the one that's the most *reliable*. In judging reliability, you've got to go on more than instinct. Here are five criteria we use in assessing reliability. Few statements meet all five criteria, but those that meet several make the strongest supports for generalizations.

1. *Accuracy*. If the source has seen an event and reported it carefully, readers assume he's also reported it accurately. Total accuracy is seldom achieved: six eyewitnesses to an

accident often give six conflicting reports. However, a report from a primary source is generally more accurate than one reported secondhand. That's one value in concentrating on primary research sources.

2. *Authenticity.* You always get authenticity automatically from a primary source, and never from a secondary source. The data has come from the horse's mouth—the logical, natural origin of the information. If you can't confirm the authority's data, be careful to present it in your paper as an authentic *statement.* Remember that it's not necessarily fact.

3. *Credibility.* Whether primary or secondary, the source's way of telling the facts and backing them up, or the source's proven track record, may lead you to conclude subjectively that the source is credible and the facts can be believed. That's how to present the information in your paper.

4. *Plausibility.* You may conclude that the fact, no matter what its source, makes sense to you. Presumably, it will to other people, too. Write it not as verified fact but as plausible consideration.

5. *Corroboration.* If you obtain the same information from two separate believable sources, it becomes a verified or corroborated fact. In that case, you've objectively demonstrated, if not the 100% accuracy, at least the honesty of your sources. It's a very strong argument for your case. In reporting the fact, it often earns extra points to give both citations.

Without a doubt, if one of your references is both the most interesting and the most reliable source of data, you've got the best of both worlds.

SHORTCUT 34

Quote Wisely

Most students use quotations like salt, sprinkling them here and there in hopes they'll liven up and lend weight to the paper. Unfortunately, a poor or dull or incomprehensible idea doesn't gain either credibility or excitement just because it's a direct quotation. You must choose your quotations as carefully as you do the rest of your citations.

Use a direct quotation only when you need the actual voice of authority for a fact or opinion, or when someone's way of saying something is important to the point or point of view of your paper. If the authority you want to cite is long-winded in his statement, throw away the quotation marks and paraphrase his words, giving him credit for the thought but not the precise content.

Whether you're paraphrasing or quoting, honesty demands that you tell whether the words have come to you firsthand or secondhand. "He told me," signals that you got the information in person right from the source. "He wrote," signals that you read the information, but it still came right from the primary source. "He was reported to say" and similar phrases signal that the quote was distilled through a second source. The reader must have this information to assess its reliability, and the grade-A paper provides it.

Whether you quote or paraphrase, put your attribution first and the information second. (Dr. Jane Jones says that hangnails are inherited. . . .) It's not only easier for the reader to follow, but it makes the information sound more convincing. If you're providing footnotes or a bibliography, you need not cite a great deal of information about the source in the text. But do include the basis of expertise. If it's a person, state her title, the agency she represents, the experience or reputation that makes her authoritative. (Dr. Kate Timmons, chair of the department of education at Southern Podunk University and author of numerous studies on classroom drowsiness, says that. . . .)

When relying on secondary sources, you must not only tell the authority's name and credentials, but state the place where you got the information. (Dr. Kate Timmons, chair of the department of education at Southern Podunk University and author of numerous studies on classroom drowsiness, was quoted by *The New York Times* as saying, "The brightest students always fall asleep in class. . . .") First, this lends credibility to your citation. Second, it helps you (or the reader) if you ever need to research the facts further.

Before you lean on testimony from any source, primary or secondary, use the following guidelines to decide whether it belongs in your paper.

1. *Are the source's facts still correct?* If they were expressed long ago, have recent facts discredited them?

2. *Is his authority still intact?* The heroes of one generation sometimes become the villains of the next.

3. *Is his statement or opinion made in a field that's within the scope of his authority?* Anwar Sadat, for example, won a Nobel Prize for peace, but that's not credential enough to quote him as a specialist in Third World economics.

4. *Is the context of your quotation accurate?* A phrase, a sentence, or even an entire paragraph taken out of context can seem to mean something entirely different from what was intended. Even a paraphrased thought can be misinterpreted if it's detached improperly from the thoughts that once surrounded it.

5. *Has the authority changed his mind?* Even a scientist refines his conclusions and evidence on the basis of new research. If you can't check with the person, you should at least state the date of the quotation clearly in your paper.

SHORTCUT 35

Paraphrase Carefully

Quotation is using the exact words of your source. Paraphrasing is rephrasing the ideas in your own words. Most students quote much too much, and make too little use of paraphrase. It's easy to know what to leave out, and what to put into your own words, if you keep in mind that, like every other part of your paper, whatever you quote should be clear, interesting, and to the point. If it's not to the point, leave it out. If it's unclear or uninteresting, rephrase it in better words.

You may find that some parts of a quotation are to the point, and the rest extraneous. If you can do so *without changing the meaning of the quotation,* just leave out the extra parts, inserting a series of three dots (. . .) wherever you delete anything. Here's an example showing how to cite, right from the previous paragraph.

> Kesselman-Turkel and Peterson said, in their book *Research Shortcuts* (Contemporary Books, 1982), "Most students . . . make too little use of paraphrase. It's easy to know . . . what to put into your own words. . . . If it's unclear or uninteresting, rephrase it in better words."

Some parts of a quotation may be interesting and well put, and others tedious or hard to understand. In that case, quote the good parts and paraphrase the rest. It's amazing how fast this surgery turns a dull paper into a zippy one. But don't chop up quotations, stringing bits and pieces together with a few linking words of your own. It distracts the eye from your point. Instead, paraphrase most or all of the quotation.

Here's *bad* paraphrasing:

> Kesselman-Turkel and Peterson say that "most students" don't paraphrase enough and that "it's easy to know" what to paraphrase: whatever's "unclear or uninteresting."

This paraphrasing is much easier to read:

> Kesselman-Turkel and Peterson say that most students don't paraphrase enough and that it's easy to know what to paraphrase: whatever's "unclear or uninteresting."

When you paraphrase, aim for economy of words. Don't ever quote a source directly and, in addition, paraphrase or summarize her words. If your source needs translation, she should not be quoted directly in the first place. Graders often assume that redundancy comes from padding: adding words to lengthen an inadequately researched paper. Often as not, when they uncover redundancy, they lower the grade.

SHORTCUT 36

Know the Fine Line between Fair Use and Plagiarism

Throughout school you're warned, "Don't plagiarize." The consequences are grim. Everybody knows that if you buy or borrow someone else's paper and turn it in as your own, that's plagiarism. But what about borrowing a source's unique idea?

How much can you borrow, and how much do you have to change something to make it your own? Few books for the student answer that question. We've seen one (*Plain English Please,* 2nd edition, by Gregory Cowan and Elisabeth McPherson) that warns, "Never use more than three consecutive words belonging to another writer without putting quotation marks around them." This guideline is sure to keep you out of trouble but, as our example of bad paraphrasing in Shortcut 34 shows, you can end up with a choppy, hard-to-read manuscript.

Here's the guideline we prefer: *Use another author's words or ideas sparingly, and only with credit, and then only if it's the best literary device available to make the point that has to be made.*

To use this guideline, you must understand the difference between *information* and *expression* and between *legality* and *ethics.*

Once it's published, *information* becomes everyone's property. Legally, anyone can freely borrow any information anyone else has collected. Ethically, it's considered proper to give credit to the collector, but so long as you do, you can borrow as much as you like. Ideas are considered in a class with information. You can borrow as many of a source's ideas as you like, but it's ethical to give credit where credit is due.

Words, on the other hand, are protected by law. You cannot copy another person's book or paper in its entirety without infringing on the author's copyright. Even if you put the book or paper in your own words, you cannot extensively copy the specific progression of ideas and examples without committing plagiarism.

Copyright law is practical, however, and recognizes that researchers need latitude in using other authors' works. Therefore, the doctrine of *fair use* has evolved. It says, in short, that you may copy for publication as much of another author's work as will not diminish its commercial value. If that seems fuzzy, it's because it was intended so; the framers of the law want folks to rely on common sense when weighing the pros and cons of borrowing someone else's words.

If you were to copy an entire paper and publish it, that would be not just plagiarism, but illegal copyright infringement. If you were to copy a few sentences from a book, that would not be. If you copy 150 words from a 20,000-word book you're legally safe—but if you hand in a 500-word paper of which 150 words are someone else's, your grade will most likely be lowered for lack of originality. To be safe, follow our italicized guideline.

You don't have to credit an author who has borrowed another person's ideas. For example, if we've written a book that sums up Einstein's ideas on relativity, and you use our book in researching a paper on modern physics, we don't expect you to mention us when discussing the theory of relativity. On the other hand, if our book suggested, "Einstein's theory of relativity changed the foundations of physics as completely as Darwin's *Origin of Species* changed those of biology," we do expect you to credit us whether you borrow just that observation or the exact words we've used.

When in doubt, be generous with your attributions. If you've researched the topic well, and have something original to say, your citations will show your confidence and intellectual strength. If you've researched poorly or have nothing new to contribute to the topic, no amount of covert borrowing is likely to get you an A.

SHORTCUT 37

Fiddle with Your First Draft

While you'd never catch a professional writer worth his salt turning in an uncorrected first draft, most students rush their papers right to school the minute the last word's been squeezed through the printer. Some don't even reread for typographical errors and spelling mistakes.

This cavalier approach (cavalier: given to offhand dismissal of important matters) is what turns grade-A research into grade-C papers. Go one step further than your peers, and fiddle with that first draft, and you'll get the grade you want. It's as simple as that.

The first step is to fill the holes you've left. This may necessitate another trip to the library or another conversation with a primary source, but often the information you need is so specific, you can get it with a phone call or an online search. Most librarians are happy to look up a quick fact in response to a phoned request.

Even if you have no holes to fill, it's a good idea to put your first draft aside for a day or two, so you have some perspective when you reread it.

Read twice. The first time, don't worry about the correct word or grammatical construction. Read for an overview. See if the organization is smooth and makes sense. Notice whether rearrangement of ideas is needed. It's the rare paper that's in its most perfect logical order the first time around. In this computerized age, rearrangement is a simple cut-and-paste job.

Take out the sets of notes from your file folder, and check through to see that you've included all the references you expected to use. If you're missing any, insert them where appropriate. Fill in where you've found weak points that need more amplification or better proof.

Once you've perfected the content of your paper, read it a second time for expression. Put in the insertions—words, phrases, or sentences—that smooth out your transitions. Check that you've chosen the best words, sentence structure, and grammar. (*The Grammar Crammer,* another book in this series, should help you here.) Turn on your spelling checker and correct misspellings—but if you use the word processor's grammar checker, use common sense in taking its advice. Grammar checkers keep getting better but they're still not always right. It's a good idea to look up any spelling, punctuation, and grammar rules that you're not sure of.

SHORTCUT 38

Print a First-Class Final Draft

No matter how objective the grader, a paper that's easy to read seems a notch better. So pay careful attention to form—and your instructor's guidelines—in preparing the final draft.

If you need to submit the paper on an electronic disk or as an e-mail attachment, make sure you know what word processing formats are acceptable. If it's wanted on paper, stick with white, unlined sixteen-pound or twenty-pound 8 ½" by 11" paper. Use only black type for everything but color illustrations. Double-space and keep margins 1 ½ inches at the left and right and at least 1 inch at the top and bottom. Unless your instructor states a preference, create an attractive cover page, centering the title on the page and putting your name under it along with the class name and other identifying information. Repeat the title, along with your name and class, at the top of all the pages of your manuscript unless you're told to do otherwise. Number all the pages.

If your paper doesn't call for footnotes, end notes, or a bibliography, be sure to substitute complete reference information in the text right where you've keyed the first draft to your bibliography sheets. If you're expected to footnote or prepare a bibliography, and you haven't been shown how, use the following method. (Unless you've specifically been told to exclude a bibliography, prepare one. It usually reaps extra points.)

A *footnote* goes at the bottom of the page on which the reference appears, often separated from the text by a line across the page. An *end note* is a footnote listed, along with the rest of your notes, at the end of your paper. (The footnoting tool in word processing programs, which can do both kinds, is a great timesaver once you learn how to use it.) If you have just a few footnotes, you can use an asterisk (*) right after the reference, even if it's in the middle of a sentence, and another asterisk at the footnote. But for most papers, footnotes are numbered consecutively. (The numbers or asterisks go after all punctuation except dashes.)

A *bibliography* groups all the references you used for your paper (whether referred to directly in the paper or not) alphabetically at the end of the paper. Though the paper may mention the author or title, these bibliography citations are neither starred nor numbered. A bibliography is often stylistically different from a list of endnotes in other ways, too. Here's a common way of listing a source in a bibliography:

Fowler, H. W. *A Dictionary of Modern English Usage,* 2nd edition. Revised by Sir Ernest Gowers. New York: Oxford University Press, 1965.

Entire handbooks have been written about proper footnoting and bibliography preparation. If your instructor is a stickler for form, or your paper's sources are complicated, we suggest you refer to the handbook that's preferred in your school. Many schools use the *Chicago Manual of Style.* You can read footnoting rules and examples from it and from several other university style manuals online.

Once your final draft has been checked, print it and read it again for typographical errors. If you find a better word here and there, make neat corrections in ink or, better still, print the page again. If a big change is needed, don't be lazy; make the revision on your computer and print the whole paper again. Hand it in—on time—and relax. You're bound to get an A.